Thriving Through Chaos

A MANUAL

*Be On Your Spiritual Grind So That
You Bounce Back Quickly From
Life's Curve Balls (and Pandemics Too 😊)*

Gillian C. Thomas

ISBN: 979-8-9866728-0-9

Cover Design by Rhea Welch
Author Photograph by Jill Vallery

This book is dedicated to:

All Spiritual Humans.

Light the Spark by Making a Start.

-- Gillian C. Thomas

"Your vision will become clear only when
you can look into your own heart.
Who looks outside, dreams; who looks inside, awakes."

-- Carl Jung

Table of Contents

Foreword

Thriving Through Chaos: A Manual is a potpourri of wisdom and insight that touches so many aspects of the body, mind, and spirit. I have read many books on healing and growth, but none have been so comprehensive, so concise, or so fascinating as this one.

It's a divine gift. Gillian C. Thomas has given a great deal of herself to this book.

It's a masterpiece. A fitting gift to humanity that can help us face the turmoil and uncertainty of these times; a reminder that despite the fear, doubt, and illness that pervade our lives, we are still capable of hope and healing. When one considers that this is her first book, it's clear to see the enormous personal sacrifice she made in order to pour so much of herself into this compilation of profound thoughts, experiences, and knowledge.

But don't take my word for it. Turn the pages, but buckle up and prepare yourself for a cosmic ride as she takes you through eight chapters, from "On Quitting a 'Perfectly Good' Job" to "Designate A Space for Connecting." And as if that wasn't enough, Part 2 is packed with tools and tips. Turning these pages will enthrall and mesmerize you, perhaps even give you pause to ponder. I assure you that you will be transformed, just as I was the first time I read this book.

I would like to segue into what I believe is the most important aspect of this Foreword, Gillian C. Thomas, the author of Thriving Through Chaos: A Manual. When I first met Gillian, I knew she was special, a creative, which she doubted at the time, and I could tell she was meant to heal and transform lives. We have been friends for 18 years, and I am a living testimony to her generosity, grace, kindness, and patience. I say with deep conviction and without hesitation that Gillian is a divine messenger. Without her, I would not have had the strength to persevere through some of the more difficult times in my life. Her calmness, compassion, and ability to see the good in others have often saved me and many others from regrettable situations, deep pain, and sorrow.

I am grateful that Gillian has taken the time and effort to pour so much of herself into this book. This is a gift to all of us, and a lesson in courage, determination, perseverance, resourcefulness, and sacrifice. We could not have asked for a more qualified conduit for this potpourri of knowledge and wisdom.

To a selfless giver with the grace and kindness of a sage: may this book be the blessing to many as it was created to be.

Much success on this literal journey, my dearest. One love!

Selwyn A. Collins, Author

Introduction

On February 14, 2020, I gave myself the perfect Valentine's Day gift. I walked away from my job with no backup plan. I had known for many years that I had to change my lifestyle, but I didn't have the courage to do so until 2020. I could no longer justify continuing to harm myself by being and doing what was not serving my highest and greatest good. My lifestyle was severely distracting me from clarifying what served my highest and greatest good.

I was completely burnt out from being in survival mode. I was dissociating and couldn't remember from task to task what I had just completed and what the outcome of that had been. I was putting on the backburner what kept me alive, like meditation, exercise, family and friends, and replacing them with ever increasing hours in the office.

I was so tense that one day I dislocated my left shoulder while reading a document at my desk.

So even though my boss kindly offered to give me a few weeks to recoup, I graciously refused. I no longer had the bandwidth for other people's rules and demands on and for my life and time. I had to disconnect completely without a return date hanging over my head.

The way we are conditioned to live and work – study hard to become qualified to work hard until we retire – never made sense to me. However, it was difficult for me to remember, and so articulate what my better way looked and felt like. Being in survival mode for so long made it easier for me to know what I didn't want. But it kept me in a cycle of getting what I didn't want. After all, what you focus on grows.

I had to quit to ease out of survival mode and meaningfully connect with myself in order to figure out my next steps.

On March 17, 2020, when everything stopped because of the pandemic, I knew that I got out just in time. The pandemic brought chaos, fear, doubt, anxiety and stress like many of us have never experienced before. So, I focused on rest and recovery despite moments of doubt and anxiety. Eventually, I found my way to Spiritual Ascension University[1], where I gained clarity, and learned how to remember who I am and what it means to be "a spiritual being having a human experience."[2] I released all doubt that I was correct in knowing that we aren't meant to work ourselves to death to pay bills and taxes. No doubt, everything I had done before this moment was preparation, but it wasn't my soul's mission. It's not your soul's mission either. Our work is to be on our spiritual paths and fearlessly immerse ourselves in our soul mission work or purpose. That's where true work-life balance lies even if you're working a 9-to-5 while on your path.

There is no black or white to this path. The foundational information might be the same for all. But it's a personalized process that is unique to you. Everything does not work for everyone in the same way, or even at all. Only you know what to do and how to do it. No one should be judging you for that or trying to convince you that their way is how it should be. Release all judgment of yourself and comparisons with others who seem to be doing it better than you, and flow.

You might be confused right now about what to do and how because you have been in survival mode for so long and cannot remember what you already know. It's like trying to recall a word that's at "the tip of your tongue." When it comes, it feels as if a piece of your puzzle fell into place. It takes work to bring that knowing to your conscious mind.

At its most basic, the work is connecting to yourself. Meditation is the easiest way to connect. If, like me, you get to a point where you need a little more formal guidance, your teacher will find you. Or you can seek out someone with whom you resonate. You'll still have to meditate though.

---

[1] www.spiritualascensionuniversity.com.

[2] Pierre Teilhard de Chardin.

For those who like to constantly gripe and complain about how bad things are, or are waiting for a savior, now is not the time. On your path you will find that complaining is pointless because you are the common denominator. Your savior is you! If you're still griping and complaining you're only telling on yourself.

If you are ready to do the work, you can try some of the tools in this book if you haven't before or revisit them if you have. There might be things that aren't discussed here that you have thought about doing. Do those, as well. At the very least, just a few minutes a day of meditation will change your outlook, physically and mentally. Trust me on that!

Your ego is not going to like the adjustments at first. You'll be doing things differently from how it's been conditioned. So, you have to tell it to stand down when it expresses discomfort, and keep going. After a while, it will recognize that you're good and that it's benefiting from all that you're doing. It's a mind game.

This work is important because when you are connecting with and improving yourself, you get bonuses like clarity on what steps you should be taking next, reduced stress, improved responses from your environment because you're no longer reacting, and improved overall health and well-being. You don't have to wait until you retire to have a good life after all!

So why write this book? I was prompted to do so around Spring 2020 while I was figuring out my next steps. I started writing from my memory, experiences, and other resources I have used. As I wrote, the rest came, including Spiritual Ascension University, to fill in the blanks with information that either clarified or provided the truth of what I already knew.

This Manual is a beginners' guide of tools and tips for those who are finding it challenging to figure out what's next and/or how to adjust to life post-March 2020.

The information is deliberately basic and general to get you started, and the tone is conversational. This is deliberate because this topic of dealing with life's challenges can be heavy. I wanted to keep things as light as possible.

The tools discussed will help you to become clear on the details of your journey. You can then choose to take that journey even though you have no idea where it ends and what will happen along the way. Trust that you will be led to other sources and resources, if necessary, that answer the questions that will arise and are not addressed here. Only you know what to do and how to do it on your journey. The point is to do the work to reveal that information. You will make discoveries about yourself that you never imagined possible, including that you already know your answers!

There will be blessings (or "blessons"), along the way, and the process will become less challenging the more you commit. You will come to see the challenging experiences as healing and enlightening blessings in your life. You will understand yourself, your relationships, and your environment. You will realize that you are not being punished. You are meant to upgrade yourself to become available to accomplish your soul's mission.

There is no right or wrong way. Just light the spark and make a start. Then keep going.

PART I: It's All On You

There are YouTube videos by well-meaning people about being on a spiritual path. Lots of them talk about doing "the work." Not many of them explain what they mean by "the work." When they do, it's vague and difficult for someone who is in survival mode to grasp.

In my experience, when you're in survival mode your connection to your intuition is minimal at best. You're therefore unable to access your inner knowing that should automatically kick in and tell you that you know what "the work" is. Even then it could be confusing and frustrating if you can't figure out where to start. It is not farfetched to think that "the work" requires a lot of stress like your 9-to-5, or involves some special secret processes available to only a very select group and that you have to pay big bucks to access. I have been there.

At its very basic, doing the work means doing what is necessary to heal yourself of traumas that keep you open to chronic stress, and close you off from having the high vibrational mindset, lifestyle and relationships, including the one with yourself, that you deserve.

One of our biggest stressors is the pandemic and its aftermath. Some continue to expect things to return to normal, meaning the way we lived before we were locked down for months beginning in March 2020. Where most of us were living in survival mode pre-pandemic, it's worse post-pandemic because we want to get back to what we defined as "normal" lives. That's not going to happen.

Fear and anxiety for the future, along with depression over what was lost as a result of the pandemic, seems to be the plague of our time. It truly doesn't have to be this way for you.

There is no going back to "normal." We are moving forward to so much better than what was. Despite what you've been told and what appears to be happening on this planet, know that you can create a life and reality of peace, joy and fulfillment for yourself. That's where we are now. All you have to do is remember that the only thing you can change is yourself by healing yourself of limiting traumas and becoming spirit-led. The rest will fall into place. That should be your normal.

In this Part of the Manual, we will talk about what it means to be in survival mode and how that way of being serves you, how to begin to heal from survival mode so that your true path becomes clearer, and how to start reclaiming your time from habits and practices that keep you in survival mode. This is some of the "the work" towards truly freeing yourself.

Ultimately, you should desire to (and will) get to the point of being able to tune into and follow your inner guidance for what's next on your journey.

Chapter One: On Quitting a "Perfectly Good" Job

I was raised to believe that you get an education toward a job/career that affords you the "luxury" of buying things as you work towards a beautiful retirement. I am not saying my upbringing was bad. It's just that our elders, and theirs before them, were conditioned to believe that success comes from giving value to others in exchange for value, and that's what they taught us. That is, you work hard for someone and follow certain rules in exchange for a salary that is supposed to satisfy your wants and needs.

Needless to say, I embraced my conditioning. I became a lawyer and transitioned into being a dutiful member of the 99% going through the motions (pun intended) required to earn money so that I can buy things and pay bills. I grew to remember that this is not exactly how life is supposed to be.

Over the years, as the tedium crept up on me, the feeling that this is not "it" settled in and grew stronger and more persistent. I started to feel tremendous resistance to my lifestyle. It manifested in adrenal fatigue and other minor health issues.

I slowly awoke to the fact that the system is deliberately set-up to work certain of us so hard that we're always in survival mode. We're not supposed to have the time to see that the value we're putting in is in no way, shape or form being reciprocated by an equitable exchange of value, unless you're willing to go all in on compromising your values. We're also not supposed to be able to focus long enough to figure out how to shift from survival mode, or even to recognize that we're in survival mode. Hence my difficulty with articulating what I want my life to be.

The way it works, regardless of whether you flip burgers in a fast-food joint or work in Mergers & Acquisitions at a white-shoe law firm or pull in a billion dollars as an entertainer, is that you work until you burn out. And then you keep working. Once you start to burn out, your ability to do the work at the pace and standard you pride yourself on starts to slip unless you abuse substances or make some other compromise to cope. Eventually, your boss notices your slip-ups and makes it seem like you're the problem.

It can make you feel crazy!

The fact is that most of the people on this planet are classified as human capital. You're valued based upon "the skills, knowledge, and experience possessed by [you as] an individual or population, viewed in terms of [your] value or cost to an organization or country."[3] This is not necessarily a bad thing. It becomes a bad thing when the one defining you cares less about your values, or values period, unless they can profit from it.

As human capital, you're nothing more than a machine for a minority to profit from. You're supposed to work mindlessly like a donkey chasing a carrot on a stick so that you never realize that you can do much, much better for yourself. Even if the thought pops into your head, you can't imagine being without a steady paycheck if you struck out on the path you're being prompted to take, especially if you have to provide for a family. Quitting seems to be an impossible option to achieve. Many of us self-medicate with television, food, pharmaceuticals and/or controlled substances.

This way of being doesn't resonate with your spirit because it's not natural. You're not a mindless machine.

> **You are not here to work hard at an unfulfilling job/career to make others happy and/or rich while you live in survival mode.**

---

[3] HUMAN CAPITAL English Definition and Meaning. *Lexico.com*. Retrieved from www.lexico.com/en/definition/human_capital.

In my experience, living in survival mode has disconnected us from who we are at our very core as the embodiments of a balance of masculine and feminine energy. The imbalance between our masculine and feminine energies creates problems for us, including the cognitive dissonance in our relationships. Women become masculinized because the system requires her to be and do in spaces that are ill-matched to her innate energy, while certain men are discouraged from embracing their feminine energy. All of this means that we are also disconnected from our Higher Self (or meta-Self).

That has been the purpose of the system we have been living in and are leaving behind. Whether you call it the patriarchy or something else, we are supposed to be so engrossed in surviving that we never have the time to remember who we are and use that knowing to thrive instead.

It doesn't matter how well compensated you are. You're a spiritual human. Your entire being starts to rebel against the system after a while. So, life as we have come to know it begins to drain you mentally, emotionally and spiritually, causing you to become physically dis-eased. If your distress gets to the point where your value to your employer diminishes too much, they simply replace you.

As I was having my experience, I knew this wasn't the life I wanted. But I had no idea how to articulate what I wanted instead because I was so stressed that all I could think of was what I didn't want. Sounds familiar?

I tried to be optimistic by being grateful and imagining that it could be worse. However, that only works in the short-term. It could only work for the long-term if my career was more aligned with my true purpose in this lifetime – my soul's mission – or was making it possible for me to work on my purpose. None of this was true for me. The work I was doing wasn't aligned with what I am here to do even though it was necessary on my path.

Would I have quit if I knew 2020 would turn out the way it did?

Absolutely!

9

It was time. I was at the point of metanoia or repentance.[4] This is when you "wake up" and recognize that something is not right with your way of life, and begin to make changes. You literally have a spiritual awakening. This is the true repentance that will save you. You know how they tell you in church to repent of your sins and be saved? Well, the "sin" is unknowingly straying from your true purpose in life. The only way to "save" yourself is to realize that you're supposed to figure out what you are here to do and get to work.

True repentance means understanding that your life should be about your spiritual growth for the highest and greatest good of all through working on yourself. This is the work that you're supposed to use your innate abilities, gifts and talents to do. Along the way, you can work at the 9 to 5 job and/or figure out how to get paid for doing what you love so that you can pay the bills.

Don't get me wrong, being on your spiritual path doesn't mean that you have to become a priest or take up residence in a lotus position on the top of a mountain in Nepal. Your soul mission work might be accomplished as you flip burgers to pay the bills. So, if that's where you are and it feels right to you, don't second guess yourself.

At my waking point, I came to understand that nothing would go right in my life if I didn't follow the prompting to quit my job. No matter how much money I made, it would never have afforded me the life I envisioned for myself.

Although "the Great Resignation" could have resulted from the vaccine mandate, I think that many who resigned are at this spiritual turning point in their lives, though they do not realize it. They may not understand that they are not meant to leverage the current job market for the next best thing where they'll end up having the same or similar experiences as before. The cycle will continue until they wise up.

---

[4] Freke, T. and Gandy, P. (2001). *Jesus and the Lost Goddess: The Secret Teachings of the Original Christians*, p. 69-70. New York, NY: Three Rivers Press.

It is important to know that being on your spiritual path is not a one-size-fits-all proposition. That is why this Manual contains basic information that applies to everyone. You have to connect to you through meditation to determine your path because your guidance comes from within. The expert on you and your life is within you.

Now, you don't have to quit your job to work on connecting and accomplishing your soul's mission. More importantly, *I'm not encouraging or advocating for anyone to quit their job.* It was something that I had to do.

If you haven't quit, or really want to but can't right now, you can still do this work. Meditate and listen for your inner guidance on what steps you need to take. If you find yourself waking up between 3 a.m. and 5 a.m. every day, use that time to meditate on the question of what's next. You're supposed to be waking at that time to meditate anyway.

·   🕊   🕊   🕊

What's Next...

In the next chapter, we'll talk a little more about metanoia and what it means when it happens for you. You have the choice to ignore how you're feeling and continue with the same old. Or you can embark on a journey of healing and self-discovery.

Chapter Two: From Metanoia to Meta-Knowing

Now, this Manual is not about how to leave your job. You don't necessarily have to quit in order to break out of survival mode. This Manual is about doing what is required to remember who you really are so that you thrive beyond the limited reality your 5 senses can perceive.

Remember that scene in the Matrix where Neo visits the Oracle? He asked her if she thinks he's the One and she punted the question back to him. She then showed him the sign above the doorway, which said "know thyself" in Latin, and explained that he would know he is the One if he was the One. In a nutshell, she believed that though he had the potential, he couldn't be the One because he lacked the knowing of self to know if he was the One. He figured it out eventually, and you can too.

For me, this process started with metanoia and continues with meta-knowing. You go from being stuck in a "got-to-get-the-bag" mindset to knowing your Self beyond the things that money can buy and the status you may have. Eventually, you meet your meta-Self or Higher Self. Your Higher Self, which is a databank of your past lives, knows everything you need to know in order to thrive regardless of the situation. So, you want to get to know yourself in order to connect with and download your inner guidance.

My understanding of metanoia is that it is an opportunity to change or transform (meta[5]) the way we think (-noia[6]) for our

---

[5] "Meta." *Merriam-Webster.com Dictionary*, Merriam-Webster, https://merriam-webster.com/dictionary/meta. Accessed 8 Oct. 2022.

[6] "Noia." *Dictionary.com*, Dictionary, https://dictionary.com/browse/-noia. Accessed 8 Oct. 2022.

spiritual betterment. I think that it's the point when your Higher Self becomes "loud" enough to override your ego and nudge you out of your comfort zone into taking the red pill[7] if you choose.

It starts with a nagging feeling that your life is not reflecting who you are and that you lack clarity of what/who is the true you. Over time, the feeling builds to a crescendo that sounds like, "I hate my life," or looks like doing self-destructive things like substance abuse to cope with stress and chaos. Maybe your life looks a like mine did. You begin to feel a strong desire for something different. This is the repentance happening.

Now is the time to pay attention to what and who comes into your life, and what they are offering. They are the responders that your desire to transform is attracting to help you. You might be tempted to reject their help if it doesn't look like what you expect.

For instance, you might reject a call that's coming through from someone you fell out with years ago not knowing they were presenting you with an opening to your next level. No regrets, though. Consider it a test to see if you're truly committed to transforming. Take it as a lesson, not a loss. That way you will be less likely to take the next opportunity at face value. This is all a part of meta-knowing or the knowing of self.

So, what is meta-knowing. The prefix "meta" has also been defined as "more comprehensive" or "transcending,"[8] while "knowing" is defined as "indicating possession of exclusive inside knowledge or information."[9] For the purposes of this Manual,

---

[7] This is a reference to the movie The Matrix where taking the blue pill allowed you to continue your life as is. The red pill, on the other hand, revealed the truth and changed your life.

[8] Id.

[9] "Knowing." *Merriam-Webster.com Dictionary*, Merriam-Webster, https://merriam-webster.com/dictionary/knowing. Accessed 8 Oct. 2022.

meta-knowing is knowledge of self that enables you to transcend the limitations that may be binding you to survival mode and empowers you to transform into someone who thrives despite life's challenges.

From my perspective, meta-knowing requires you to dig really deep within yourself and embrace what you find; even the things that you don't like about yourself. Only by embracing them will you know what you need to heal and can you begin to work on yourself and create a more fulfilling reality for yourself. Instead of blaming your parents, siblings, boss or "the man" for the state of your life, you examine yourself and learn why you can't seem to break out of your loop of screaming at your child every time they ask you a question, for instance. This is called shadow work.

Shadow work means facing down your limiting beliefs and behaviors that you prefer to hide from yourself[10] (or your shadow self) and the unhealed childhood traumas – all of the things that make you feel doubtful, guilty and ashamed. It is very uncomfortable to do in the beginning. Let's say you observe someone interacting with their child and realize that the way you behave with yours is appalling. Avoiding the discomfort is not the answer. You have to understand that your reaction to your child is triggered by your own trauma that occurred probably in your childhood. The time has come to examine why you are being triggered and to do the work to heal yourself and stop traumatizing your child.

The more you work on yourself, the easier it becomes until you are playing a game of "what's next?" because of the magic that opens up for you from pushing through. On top of that, you will learn a lot about yourself and your life, and become a more joyful person with access to everything you need to change your life for the better, if that's what you want.

---

[10] I say "yourself" because most often others can see right through you. You're only fooling yourself.

Meet Your Meta-Self

In my experience with doing my own work, the most interesting thing about working on yourself is that when you commit to revealing, facing and healing, your shadow self becomes your biggest ally.

See, based on my experience, I believe that our shadow selves are a bit like neglected children. In a sense, it is because a part of your shadow self is your wounded inner child. As you work on healing your shadow self, you're acknowledging, nurturing and allowing it to be free. In turn, it rewards you by going from being reactive and restrictive to being supportive. It gives you a heads up when you're being triggered and reminds you how to respond mindfully, instead of throwing the tantrums it used to when you hid from it.

It seems that when you acknowledge and heal your shadow self, it no longer has to "act up" to get your attention, and your meta-Self begins to emerge.

Your meta-Self is you at a level of self-awareness and functioning that helps you either to avoid or to easily overcome chaos. You're free to look around and flow in the moment because you're no longer in the tight grip of being triggered into fight, flight or freeze mode because you're afraid to let others see you.

Imagine knowing your Self beyond anything you could have ever envisioned. Imagine feeling lighter, being able to sustain joy in your life, having greater clarity, resiliency and discernment, seeing big improvements in your relationships, and being clear on why you are here. Imagine really liking and loving yourself. Imagine it all expanding and opening up more of yourself to you as you continue to do the work. Ultimately, you can easily articulate what you want, which means that you're no longer just surviving. These are only some of the benefits given that we are all individuals and our experiences will vary.

You are here to heal yourself so that you can meet your meta-Self and begin to live the mission you came here to fulfill. Healing is a continuous process. Whenever you feel triggered, something is coming up to be healed. You will meet progressively more of your meta-Self if you commit to the process. Otherwise, you'll recycle the same chaotic experiences. The choice is yours.

What's Next...

The point of being on your spiritual grind is to heal so that your physical and spiritual selves can reconnect, allowing you to determine and fulfill your soul's mission. Your chakras are the gateways that connect your physical and spiritual selves. Traumatic events (that evoke a harmful emotional response in you) create distance between the physical and spiritual. You can reconnect them with focused chakra work and by doing other things that resonate with you.

In the next chapter, we will discuss basic information about the chakras. Appendix III of this Manual contains a chakra chart, and there are many books and videos on chakras that you can research.

Chapter Three: You Are the One

Just like Neo in the Matrix, you have to learn that being "the One" is an inside job. As difficult as it might be to digest, you create your reality. To be clear, you are completely responsible for what manifests in your life. You chose to be here to have the experiences you have had or are having because you have to heal yourself and learn what you need in order to heal others. Your reality manifests from your experiences, usually in your childhood, that follow you through life and cause you to cycle through patterns of behaviors, beliefs, habits and traits.

It would be nice if you could have a perfect, trauma-free life so that your patterns are productive. Unfortunately, not all of your childhood experiences were pleasurable. You might only remember the good parts of your childhood. But some event(s) happened, and you felt and are holding on to emotions like fear, anger, sadness, guilt, shame or regret. These are harmful emotional responses that, if not dealt with when they occur, prevent you from reaching your full potential.

Your experiences were traumatic even if your sole connection to an event is as a witness. Let's say your mother had a miscarriage when you were 6 years old. That event had an effect on you from many perspectives beginning with the fact that she was pregnant and preparing to have a baby, and then suddenly she wasn't pregnant anymore, but there was no baby, and no one took the time to explain what happened. Later on, that trauma shows up in your life until you face it and heal from it. For instance, you might be a woman who wants no children and is afraid of being in a committed romantic relationship, or you might become anxious whenever you see a pregnant woman.

The good news is that you can heal yourself.

Healing doesn't mean that you will change your mind about having children. It means that you know why these patterns are occurring and can free yourself from them. This will create room for your physical and spiritual selves to connect so that your meta-Self can begin to emerge. The more traumas you heal, the more room opens up and the more solid your connection to yourself becomes.

Healing yourself involves shifts in your mindset, incorporating practices and tools that resonate, and possibly substances derived from animal and plant sources that our ancestors have used since ancient times. In my experience, while these processes can boost the growth and development of your body, mind and spirit, they do not replace the need for and benefit of focused chakra healing work to properly connect with your spiritual self.

Your unhealed traumas and their debris (the patterns, limiting beliefs and destructive behaviors they cause) take up space in your body that affects your chakras. Chakra literally means wheel in an ancient Indian language called Sanskrit. In the human body, they are constantly spinning wheels of energy that connect your physical and spiritual selves. The faster they spin the healthier they are and the easier it is to connect to your Higher Self (or meta-Self), and *vice versa*. Your unhealed traumas and their debris slow their spin. You want to heal so that your chakras spin faster and you can have a spiritual connection with yourself.

There are other important reasons that you want to heal. Your chakras are related to the organs, tissues and body systems that your traumas occupy. You can develop physical dis-eases in them if the traumas are unhealed. Dis-ease also can manifest as emotional, mental and spiritual issues. Conditions like thyroid dysfunction and fibroids are symptoms of unhealed trauma that are affecting how your chakras function. The most important reason for healing your chakras is that you won't truly know yourself until you heal and the debris is cleared.

There is estimated to be thousands of chakras in the body. This discussion is to give you a basic understanding of the 7 main ones that are located at the center of your body from the base of your spine to the crown of your head.[11] They are from lower to upper:

- Root chakra, which is at the base of your spine, and pertains to your survival, security and stability;
- Sacral chakra, about two inches below the navel, and the source of your creativity and sexual energy;
- Solar plexus chakra, between your navel and your abdomen below your sternum. It influences your personality, self-confidence, self-esteem and self-worth;
- Heart chakra, at your thymus approximately 2 fingers below your collar bone. It is the love zone of your body;
- Throat chakra, at your thyroid or Adam's apple. You speak your truth and communicate authentically from here;
- Third eye chakra, located between your brows, and links you to your intuition and imagination; and
- Crown chakra, at the top of the head, that connects you to your Higher Self and soul's mission.

As you can see, the three lower chakras (root, sacral and solar plexus) pertain to your physical (worldly) needs, while the three upper chakras (throat, third eye and crown) pertain to your spiritual needs. Your heart chakra connects the upper and lower

---

[11] Specific information on each chakra, including the corresponding organs, tissues and body systems, and related dis-eases, as well as the colors, elements, crystals, sounds, and mantras pertaining to each one, is provided in the chakra chart in Appendix III.

chakras. It also is the last one to heal completely because your heart cannot properly heal if you have traumas to be healed. It bears repeating that healing is a lifelong process, but the process is easier each time you do it.

In a sense, metanoia is a sign that you need to make some changes in your life and heal so that you can connect with your Higher Self. It brings you present to the fact that there are reasons why you have created the unfulfilling reality that you're living and that it's time to upgrade yourself. You wouldn't be giving your all to an unrewarding career if you knew who you were. Instead, you would know that your innate abilities, gifts and talents are how you make your living and thrive as you fulfill your purpose.

When you begin to take responsibility for yourself like we discuss in this Manual, you begin to heal your chakras. There are various processes for focused chakra healing depending who you reference. Typically, there are specific colors, elements, crystals, sounds, and affirmations that resonate with each chakra that are used to heal that chakra. You can also research how you can add herbs, movement, music and breath-work, to name a few, to your chakra healing practice.[12]

You might realize that a prayer you say regularly could be used to heal your chakras. For instance, Psalm 23 resonates as a chakra healing mantra given that it indirectly references the basic properties of each chakra. As you recite the Psalm, you can visualize white light rising from your root to your crown.

Having trouble creating affirmations for each chakra? How about allowing yourself to be/have the quality that the chakra represents. So, while visualizing each chakra, you can recite the following:

---

[12] Adrienne, The Chakra Doc, offers chakra healing consultations and teas through her website, https://thechakradoc.com.

- 🕊 I allow myself to be safe and secure with a solid foundation.

- 🕊 I allow myself to be creative and healthy and balanced in my sexual expression.

- 🕊 I allow myself to be confident, and have healthy self-esteem and self-worth.

- 🕊 I allow myself to open my heart to give and receive love, joy and peace.

- 🕊 I allow myself to speak my truth, listen actively, and communicate authentically.

- 🕊 I allow myself to access my intuition and inner guidance.

- 🕊 I allow myself to connect with my Higher Self, Spirit and my purpose.

Like Neo, you're the One for what you are here to do and learn. You can call it your purpose or your soul's mission or whatever term you want to use. Deep down, you know that you're here to do more than your career or job. You won't have clarity on what that is until you connect with yourself, and learn who you truly are.

Maybe some people were raised in environments that helped them to retain their memory of who they are and maintain their sense of self despite life's ups and downs. If you're not one of those people, you are responsible for healing your chakras. When they are able to spin fast enough, you can rise above being bogged down by figuring out how to survive and connect with your Higher Self (or meta-Self), which is your means for thriving.

In hindsight, you might find that everything that you've done in your life so far was leading you to your mission. If you experience metanoia, you've exhausted what those things can do for you and need to level up. Now is the time for greater focus on your journey. Along the way, you get to meet your meta-Self and connect at progressively deeper levels. Uncovering and integrating your meta-Self is a piece of the puzzle that helps you to thrive.

Your Higher Self, which is a databank of your past lives, knows everything you need to know in order to accomplish your mission. You are the only one with that specific mission. Your Higher Self can guide you through any situation you might encounter on the way. Struggling is not a thing when you're tapping into your Higher Self. So, you want to connect in order to download from your inner guidance.

The journey to becoming your version of "the One" is challenging. It takes courage to face yourself and time to work through your traumas. The important things are your perspective and your response. When you are triggered, remember that you're simply being alerted to trauma that needs to be healed. Focused chakra healing will help. But you also have to take responsibility for yourself. We will continue this discussion with how you can begin to do that.

꙳   ꙳   ꙳

What's Next...

Some people's challenges are more demanding than others. Admittedly, it is not easy to be positive and measured in our response when we believe that we have been wronged. It takes courage to face yourself and time to work through your traumas.

In the next chapter, we will talk about how stress can affect you. I'll break down how stress works and how you can start to manage yours to avoid or alleviate physical, mental, emotional and spiritual dis-ease that's slowing down your chakras.

Chapter Four: You Can't Control What's Happening, But You Can Be Mindful of Your Response to It

By now you should have realized that it is natural for us to be challenged by life. However, everyone's challenges are different. When you stop feeling sorry for yourself long enough, you realize that there are others who are much worse off than you, and even more people who are worse off than them. It's okay to compare yourself with those who are worse off than you. Not to gloat, but to maintain your perspective so that you can focus on finding your solutions. When you're able to see that things could be worse for you, it's easier to relax and flow. This is the universal Law of Relativity in a nutshell.

Timothy Freke and Peter Gandy remind us that "[s]uffering and joy are the 'stick and carrot' which goad and cajole us along the path of life."[13] In the carrot and stick story, a stubborn donkey refused to work. So, the farmer dangled a carrot on a stick just enough out of its mouth's reach that the donkey did the work while it was focused on getting to the carrot. This, in essence, is how life works in survival mode. The stick is the promise of a paycheck (the carrot) if you work hard and long enough. You can recognize it as a game and play with a sense of humor so that you get to overcome the "suffering" progressively easier and quicker. For most of us the humor is clouded by the stress of having to live outside of who we truly are.

Clearly, stress is inevitable. How you respond to stress is what's important. Constantly fearing, worrying about, and reacting to what you can't control puts you in survival mode leading to dis-

---

[13] Freke, T. and Gandy, P. (2001). *Jesus and the Lost Goddess: The Secret Teachings of the Original Christians*, p. 169. New York, NY: Three Rivers Press.

ease. You're more likely to receive what you don't want because that's all you can think/talk about.

Under stress, you're more susceptible to illness and an early death unless you understand why those are your circumstances. That is, life's challenges lead you to where you choose to save yourself by taking the time to work on yourself.

In order to develop your sense of humor for life, you'll have to do some work. While you're doing your work, effective stress management is important so that you're more likely to think before you act. Knowing the mechanics of stress in your body will help you to understand why.

Your body has an innate intelligence that helps you to manage stress when you allow it.[14] Your adrenal glands (that sit on top of your kidneys) influence your reproduction, appetite, blood sugar, stress management, growth and digestion. The adrenals produce hormones, including cortisol (the main stress hormone), adrenaline and norepinephrine (the hormones that give your body the oomph it needs to run from danger or stay and fight), and dopamine (the feel-good hormone). These and other hormones released by the adrenals regulate the levels of salt, sugar, and sex hormones released in your body. Healthy adrenals are necessary for optimal health and wellbeing.

Here's a breakdown of the stress process:

> Your boss yells at you in front of the entire office for miscalculating some important numbers. It wasn't your fault. You're pissed and embarrassed, and you're feeling all kinds of emotions. You want to get as far away from the office as possible. The stress causes your adrenals to release cortisol, adrenaline and norepinephrine (C.A.N.) so that you can flee or fight because your brain thinks you're in danger.

---

[14] Ruscio, Michael. When Your Brain is Stuck in Fight or Flight Mode. (2019, April 29). *Dr.Ruscio Blog.* Retrieved from https://drruscio.com/brain-stuck-in-fight-or-flight-mode.

❧ As your adrenals release C.A.N., your heart rate, blood pressure and blood sugar increase so that you have the energy to fight or flee, and your immune response, along with your muscle and protein levels, decreases.

❧ As you experience that stress, your body switches focus from regulating your reproductive processes, appetite, blood sugar and pressure, cognition, growth and digestion, to helping you deal with the crisis you're experiencing.

❧ If your stress is short-term and/or you handle it effectively, everything returns to normal. C.A.N. levels go back to normal functioning, and so does your body.

❧ But you can't forget what happened. On top of that, your boss keeps finding things wrong with your work, your spouse is unsupportive, your diet sucks, and you're experiencing other challenges. So, your stress becomes chronic. You're therefore constantly releasing C.A.N. because your brain believes that you are in constant physical danger. It can't tell the difference between physical danger and your work-related stress (although it can be argued that you are in physical danger from the effects of your stressors).

❧ Under chronic stress, you eventually start to have low libido and you may have trouble conceiving or experience erectile dysfunction; your menstrual cycle may become irregular; your wounds won't heal properly, if at all; you get the flu more often; you can become diabetic and/or hypertensive; you gain abdominal weight, suffer bone loss, and develop depression and stomach ulcers, among other things; and you may develop chronic fatigue.

❧ When your adrenals remain in crisis mode, your body places all of its efforts into helping you deal with your chronic stress by removing resources from vital bodily functions to those systems that allow you to run, fight or freeze in the face of danger. See, that's why you can't seem to get any work done when you're stressed![5] Your brain literally cannot function because it's not getting the proper blood supply!

This stress process is why you have to work on how you respond to your challenges. You can train yourself to pause and think about how to respond when you're under pressure instead of automatically reacting every time. Reacting thoughtlessly will only add more stress.

One definition of mindfulness is "the self-regulation of attention with an attitude of curiosity, openness, and acceptance."[16] Mindfulness invites you to observe what is happening around you without absorbing it and reacting thoughtlessly.

Practices that encourage mindfulness such as yoga, meditation and breathwork have been described as "New Age." But they are ancient practices passed down to us by our ancestors. The ancient Egyptians practiced yoga as seen in hieroglyphs and artifacts from that era, including those found in King Tutankhamen's tomb.[17]

You're mindful when you're viewing your actions, thoughts and feelings objectively, acknowledging how you feel, examining why you feel that way, and formulating effective and sustainable

---

[5] Deloitte conducted a survey on employee burnout that involved 1,000 full-time US professional. Ninety-one percent of them, including those who were "passionate" about their jobs, reported that high stress levels reduced their quality of work. Workplace Burnout Survey. *Deloitte*. Retrieved from www.deloitte.com/us/en/pages/about-deloitte/articles/burnout-survey.html.

[16] Nlemlec, R.M. (2017, Nov. 1). 3 Definitions of Mindfulness That Might Surprise You. *Psychology Today*. Retrieved from https://www.psychologytoday.com/us/blog/what-matters-most/201711/3-definitions-mindfulness-might-surprise-you.

[17] Hotep, Yirser Ra. (2016, October 26). Kemetic Yoga: Resurrection of an African Legacy. *Gaia*. Retrieved from www.gaia.com/article/kemetic-yoga; https://kemeticyogaskills.com/history-of-kemetic-yoga/.

solutions. Knowing that you can handle the stressful situation you encounter helps you to become present to how you respond to your environment. You can adjust your perspective in a way that supports your health and well-being, becoming better able to withstand pressure like the diamond you are. When you train yourself to live this way, you stop projecting your trauma onto other people and begin to heal yourself because you remember that the challenges you experience are meant to trigger you to do your healing work.

Cultivating mindfulness requires a deep dive into yourself that is not easy to do because you have to make an honest self-assessment and you won't like what is revealed. You have to face your shadow, i.e., all of the aspects of yourself that you don't like and make you cringe – your thoughts, emotions, previous actions and experiences. It's tempting to run back to the safety of avoidance. But you will learn that when you continue to face yourself, life gets better and you begin to enjoy the reveal-and-heal process. This is when you start to see your "suffering" as mere challenges to be overcome. Life eventually seems less oppressive and easier to face.

Challenges become easier to deal with and you will have decreased stress, anxiety and depression when you're mindful.[18] You realize that blaming others, your environment and your circumstances, and expecting them to change for you will get you nowhere. You learn that the only thing you can control/change is yourself, and that working on yourself is what brings about the change you want.

The best thing about being mindful is that the self-assessment process becomes easier each time you have to do it and you start to level up in subtle ways. For instance, you might notice that when you glance at a mirror, your reflection smiles back at you instead of your usual frown. You will even find that the rewards (or

---

[18] Mindfulness. *Psychology Today.* Retrieved from https://www.psychologytoday.com/us/basics/mindfulness.

the carrot) that you get from doing this work makes you feel so jubilant that you get through each new challenge with less stress.

People will pick up on the changes in you and you'll notice their attitude change toward you. More telling, is that as your true essence (your meta-Self) shines through, people who never paid much attention to you before now want to know and be around you. They sense the change in you even if they (and you) are not yet aware of what's actually happening. You will think that the people around you changed when all that happened is that you worked on yourself and shifted.

Your friends-in-negativity might disappear from your life because the "new you" no longer exists in that reality. Don't feel badly about that or their accusations that you've changed and think you're better than them. It is inevitable because you have upgraded yourself and they are still in the old reality. Remember "those who insist in dragging you into the past, threaten your present, and can assassinate your future."[19] Stay true to who you are becoming. Some of them will return. Those who don't are not meant to.

There's no need to be embarrassed about things your old self did/said/thought, or for being a jerk to your family and friends for most of your adult life. You might need to make amends though. This doesn't mean that the people you offended will want to forgive you. Just remember that everything is relative, and that there's a "good" side and a "bad" side to everything.[20] Focusing on the bad brings more of the same. Forgive yourself.

This may sound cheesy, but life really gets easier when you do this work. It doesn't mean that you will never again be stressed, or that you should be anyone's doormat. You learn, however, to be mindful about where you choose to place your attention. For instance, is it really worthwhile to spend hours watching the anchors on your favorite news channel rehash the same stories over

---

[19] Collins, Selwyn A. (2011). *The EartHeart Knows*, p. 148. Brooklyn, NY: https://eartheartknows.selco2000.com.

[20] This is the Law of Polarity.

and over again as you yell at your TV and plunge deeper into anxiety and depression?

Once you understand that the only thing you can control is yourself, life becomes easier. You'll be more inclined to live in a way that preserves your health and well-being. Don't worry about being called selfish. What is selfish is what you inflict on yourself and the people in your life when you routinely allow events outside of yourself to control and frustrate you.

It is true that many people face challenges where they need the support of a licensed medical and/or mental health professional. You can continue to receive that support as you do this work. You also can work with practitioners of alternative healing modalities to get to the root of your problems instead of covering up your symptoms with medication and/or controlled substances. You'll be surprised at how much faster you'll heal.

If you're someone who tends to overthink things, it might be helpful to remember to follow your inner guidance when this work becomes challenging. Your left brain is your thinking, more verbal, logical side that houses your ego. This is where most of the "chatter" comes from. On the other hand, your right brain is your creative side that houses your intuition and is less verbal. If you're overthinking this process, those thoughts could be from your left brain. You can try switching your focus to your right brain for a little while to see if that helps you to calm down and hear beneficial solutions to the challenges you're facing. This works for me.

It is important to show yourself love and compassion as you do this work. You will slip into old patterns because you have been one way for most of your life. Your ego prefers the old you because it's familiar. Rather than beating yourself up, have a good laugh at yourself (or cry for not more than 10 minutes). After that, breathe, take responsibility for your actions, and make a mental note to do better next time, and the next, until you develop an awareness that is second nature. Eventually you'll be able to nimbly side-step your old programming until it's no longer an issue.

What's Next...

In the next chapter, we will talk about how we create the very things we say/think we don't want through our speech and thoughts, and how to begin to train yourself to do the opposite.

Chapter Five: What Are You Saying and Thinking and Feeling?

Very important in life, and especially on your spiritual path, are what you're saying, thinking and feeling. You get back what you put out through your words, thoughts and emotions. This means that your thoughts generate emotions (and vice versa) that cause you to say and do, things, or not, which bring about the outcomes that you see in your life. To put it another way, your thoughts turn into things. To overcome this pattern, you have to work your way out of survival mode so you can stop calling into being what you don't want. Maintaining a mindset that helps you to create wonders is a muscle that you build just as if you're building your triceps in the gym.

Be mindful of what you say and think about yourself, others, and your life in general to avoid recycling into survival mode. You can rise above negative circumstances and/or environments you desire to change by choosing to see the positive in them as much as possible.

The universal Law of Polarity reminds us that everything is dual, meaning that everything has an opposite (or that there are two sides to everything). None is better or worse than the other. It's all relative to your perspective. Knowing this, you can choose to see the bus you missed as a problem or as a potential blessing. In the moment, it might not make sense because you're late for an appointment. So, you take the next bus and see that the bus you missed is stalled because another vehicle hit it. You could have ended up in the hospital with no idea of when you would have been healthy enough to reschedule that missed appointment. Instead, you arrive at your appointment on time and the person you're meeting with isn't ready to see you as yet.

How do you create through your thoughts and sayings? Here are a couple of scenarios:

1. Let's say you're on the NYC subway and the train you're on is moving along at a nice rate, but you're antsy about making a 9:00 a.m. appointment on time. You start to think/say things like, "I hope this train doesn't slow down" or "Something always happens to make me late when I'm on the subway." All of a sudden, the conductor announces that there is heavy train traffic ahead and the train starts to move very slowly until it gets to your stop. Of course, you're late. It's not a coincidence. You created that outcome with your powerful self.

2. You adopt a catchy nickname that reflects that you always seem to get into trouble. And you continue to always get into trouble. Coincidence? I don't think so. It could be that your nickname is amplifying your thoughts about yourself and people's responses to you and trouble is all you'll see unless you stop using that name.

It might be hard to accept that your thoughts/words manifest in your life circumstances that we call coincidences, or even that you created the reality you find yourself in. But your thoughts and words shape how you're feeling, and you project that feeling causing the very thing you don't want to materialize. Start to pay attention to what happens when you speak or think and evoke the corresponding emotion, and you'll see this is true.

Learning how to be mindful of your words and thoughts helps you to break your tendency to create what you don't want. For instance, instead of saying that you're "struggling" with a situation, you can say that you're being "challenged" by it. "Struggle" implies violence, while a challenge seems easier to deal with and overcome.

Similarly, instead of giving yourself damaging feedback like "I can't do anything right!" or "nothing ever goes right for me," or calling yourself "stupid," you can use constructive language, which by definition will build you up. For example, you can say, "That didn't go how I wanted it to. How can I do better next time?"

Another thing to do if you're in victim mode is to repeat inspiring affirmations to yourself to raise your vibration. When you acknowledge enough times that the opposite of your low emotions/thoughts/feelings is true, thinking and speaking in that way could become an automatic shift for you each time you realize you're in victim mode.

Now apply all of the above to your relationships and the people you encounter throughout your day. You won't be able to avoid extending your new way of being to them, anyway. Once you open up to the benefits of adjusting your behavior, your improved state of being will automatically project to those you come into contact with.

I have learned through experience that training yourself to generate constructive and productive emotions, thoughts and words, programs your cells to vibrate at a higher level. You then emit the kind of energy that attracts positivity to you.

Think of how your body feels when you or someone else talks down to you or insults you. You sort of shrink and feel badly about yourself. You also have physiological changes like an elevated heart rate or blood pressure. Well, if you're constantly telling yourself destructive things, you're doing the same thing to yourself. Imagine what this is doing to your body. Imagine what you're doing to others when you do the same to them.

This doesn't mean that you won't have challenges that bring you to a dark place and/or that you should ignore your problems. It means that you build yourself up to where you are more inclined to acknowledge how you are feeling and create viable solutions that help you to move on quickly. This way you're not constantly wallowing in the energy of fear, doubt and anxiety.

It means that you learn to recognize that you're being triggered so that you can examine why instead of reacting only to find out that you overreacted.

So be kind to yourself so that you can extend the same to others.

What's Next...

In the next few chapters, we will discuss important areas of your life where what and how you feed your mind matters for developing mindfulness, and for having the thoughts, feeling and words that generate high vibrational outcomes in your life.

Chapter Six: Put the Media on Time-Out

It seems that broadcast media generates the same fear-inducing and soul-depleting "news" over and over again 24/7. The same can be said for some television shows (both dramas and sitcoms) that depict current events in their story lines. And then there's social media where people share opinions, theories and information that can generate fear, anxiety and depression.

When you're working on upgrading yourself, depending on your physiological response to the media, it might be best to tune out of the media until you're able to observe without absorbing what you're seeing.

Some people can experience the media with objectivity and a sense of humor. Others cannot. Your physiological response is reflected in what happens in your body as you view the content on the television and other media.

- Does the news make you feel anxious and depressed?

- Does your heart beat faster when you watch reality TV shows?

- Do you breathe shallower than usual when watching certain shows?

- Do you yell at the television?

- Are you constantly thinking about or discussing with others the latest "unbelievable" thing that happened?

You may have an uncomfortable sensation in your stomach/solar plexus area, which erodes your confidence in yourself to withstand your challenges and reinforces the myth that you have no control over your reality. None of this is healthy for you. These are all signs that what you're watching is affecting you on a cellular, and contributing to your stress.

Chronic exposure to media images of gloom and doom affects you physiologically. All of your bodily functions, including your nervous, metabolic and digestive systems react in some way when they sense the effect on you of what you're consuming. Post-9/11 studies indicated that exposure to media images of the 9/11 events had significant impact on people's physical and psychological health.[21]

You're in chronic fight or flight or freeze mode, which as we discussed in Chapter Two, can cause physical and mental health issues if not brought under control.[22] Your body is so well designed that it knows when it is being exposed to stimuli that is harmful to your DNA and has to work on counteracting the effects. So, when you are on a constant loop of negative television programming, your body releases neurotoxins. The explanation is that your body recognizes the information you're receiving is false and wants nothing to do with it.[23]

Doesn't this sound like the stress response we talked about in Chapter Four?

And by the way, this false information can come from anything in your environment, including the food you consume.

---

[21] Silver, R.C., et al. (Psychol Sci. 2013 Sep.). Mental – and physical – health effects of acute exposure to media images of the Septermber 11, 2001, attacks and the Iraq War. *PubMed.gov*. Retrieved from www.pubmed.ncbi.nlm.nih.gov/23907546/.

[22] What Happens to Your Body During the Fight or Flight Response? Your Survival Response Explained. *Cleveland Clinic*. Retrieved from https://health.clevelandclinic.org/what-happens-to-your-body-during-the-fight-or-flight-response/; Ruscio, Michael. (2019, April 29). When Your Brain is Stuck in Fight or Flight Mode. *Dr. Ruscio Blog*. Retrieved from https://drruscio.com/brain-stuck-in-fight-or-flight-mode/.

[23] Morris, Yao Nyamekye. (2008). *Awakening the Master Masculine*, p. 136. Atlanta, GA: Grand Trine Productions & Black River Press.

You may have heard the term, "the issue is in the tissues." This means that everything you take into your body is processed by it, even negative information from the media. Your body doesn't want in it what doesn't resonate with it and help it to be healthy. Unfortunately, you inadvertently attack your body through this media exposure by creating the environment that allows it to release neurotoxins that are harmful to your mental, physical and spiritual health. The opposite of this process occurs when you give your body what it resonates with.

It may be true that the media's job is to keep us informed. But do you really need to constantly immerse yourself in that energy day in and day out?

A lot of the time you don't even need to know what's being reported because it is completely irrelevant to you in the grand scheme of things. It's there to distract you and keep you vested in an unsupportive system. Essentially, being on a constant information loop distracts you from creating a reality that feeds you instead of one that's constantly taking from you and leaving you depleted.

You can simply tune out if the information you're receiving is keeping you in harmful emotional states. Trust me. You're not missing anything.

Tuning out might not be easy at first. There are daily and weekly shows that you like to watch and you need to know what will happen to your favorite characters on the next episodes. You feel like you'll be missing out. But when you finally pull the plug and realize what you could have been doing with your time, you will be happy that you tuned out.

Most of all, you'll understand that you're not missing anything. And if you do, someone you know will likely fill you in even if you don't care to know.

What's Next...

Next, we will talk about how disconnecting from the media opens you up to seeing the possibilities for making improvements in yourself and your life and increasing your potential for obtaining positive outcomes and successful solutions.

Chapter Seven: See Possibilities in the Chaos

Believe it or not, you can thrive in times of chaos. This is easier to see when you are not always glued to your television or computer screen. You are more likely to act upon the ideas that you receive when you are not distracted by the media.

There are people who always seem to do well regardless of the circumstances. Then there are people who unexpectedly and against all odds rise above the difficulties they're facing and succeed beyond their wildest imagination. If you're on social media, you're probably aware that many people were able to create and maintain successful businesses throughout the pandemic in 2020. The Los Angeles Times reported that "[t]he pandemic saw a boom in new Black-owned businesses – the largest surge in the last quarter-century."[24] You probably know (or are) one of these people.

Maybe these new business owners created their success even though they were following the minutiae of the pandemic news. But I doubt that.

The important thing is to understand that even in the midst of challenges there is potential for changing your reality. One of the things that can happen is that you tap into your innate abilities, gifts and talents that you overlooked while in survival mode. Just because you're on a spiritual path doesn't mean that you are not supposed to benefit financially and otherwise from using your gifts, talents and abilities. What if your spiritual path involves creating an herbal product that allows people to heal from a specific health

---

[24] Lee, D. (2021, June 28). The pandemic saw a boom in new Black-owned businesses – the largest surge in the last quarter-century. *Los Angeles Times*. Retrieved from www.latimes.com/politics/story/2021-06-28/pandemic-silver-lining-black-owned-business-startups-surge-to-25-year-high.

condition without the trauma of surgery and pharmaceutical drugs?

This is why it pays to avoid impractical uses of your time. Sitting quietly with your thoughts does not fall into this category. In your quiet moments you might be prompted to write a book, develop a never before seen product, or start the business you've always dreamt of owning. You probably shouldn't dismiss that prompt you receive even if current events seem to say "now is not the time." Your intuition (connection to divinity) is telling you the opposite. You can miss out on being successfully self-employed if you don't pay attention.

I can't think of anyone who would pass up on being their own boss if the opportunity came to them tied up in a neat package. The thing is that you have to work for that package. Just not as hard as you think. You have to pay attention and follow your promptings even though they might seem crazy and impossible for you to accomplish.

If you're getting ideas about how you can earn a substantial income even though the world seems to be crumbling around you, trust that what's happening in the world is not your reality. Instead, you're supposed to tune into to your ideas and follow the directions you're receiving to make your ideas manifest. As long as you're not abusing your power in the process, you'll be fine.

Even if you're not being prompted to do something specific, there could be something you've wanted to do or be before you settled for your current career. What was that thing? You can ask yourself questions like:

- What are my gifts, talents and abilities?

- What do people seek me out for the most?

- How can I use these qualities to improve my life and the lives of the people in my community?

This is all part of your spiritual journey. You just have to stop ignoring the cosmic nudges and tune in.

What's Next...

In the next chapter, we will talk about where you can find information that is unique to you, that can help you to rise above chaotic times. Let's talk about the blueprint for your life next.

Chapter Eight: Get to Know Your Life's Blueprint

There is a building boom in New York City. All across the City, new structures are being erected. The building process involves an architect who creates a plan or blueprint for how the building will look inside and out. For that matter, even a basic shack has a blueprint of sorts because the builder has to know where to put windows and doors, what areas will be designated for cooking and sleeping, and so on.

Similarly, you came into this dimension with a blueprint for your life based on your date, place and time of birth. That blueprint, your Natal (or Birth) Chart, proves that you're not meant to struggle and live in survival mode while you strive to fulfill your role as human capital.[25] [26] Your natal chart is significant if you're at the point where your life in survival mode no longer makes sense.

Your natal chart is unique to you as it is based on the alignment of the sun, moon and certain other planets with the 12 astrological signs (and the 12 houses the astrological signs represent) at the date, place and time you were born. You might share the same birth date, place and time with others. However, you will each have differences in your natal charts that are unique to you, and account for the differences in your characters and life's journeys.

Your natal chart clues you in on past life experiences that are relevant to you in this lifetime, why you are the way you are, why it's okay to be who you are as long as you're not abusing your

---

[25] Anthony, Kyree. (2020). How to Read Natal Charts Easily and Effectively; Understanding your birth chart in your own language. A Workbook. San Bernardino, CA.

[26] Anthony, Kyree. (2020). Astrology Explained: How to use Imagination to Understand Astrology at an Intimate Level. Monee, IL.

power, the trauma(s) you have to heal and how to heal them, your soul's mission, your strengths and weaknesses, and so on.

Although all of this might sound farfetched, if you ever have an opportunity to review your natal chart you will realize that the information resonates because you have already experienced some of the things reflected in it. Your natal chart validates why every fiber of your being is screaming at this very moment, "I DON'T WANT TO DO THIS ANYMORE," even though you're excellent at your job. Now you know why your life took a certain trajectory and then stagnated.

Having a deeper understanding of my personal astrology helped me to understand why my lifestyle was so unsettling. For instance, I was born a Libra, so I need my life to be balanced. My career choice doesn't lend itself to balance. To top it off, key placements in my chart showed me that I was working against my interests. No wonder I was in survival mode.

Would I have made different choices had I understood my chart earlier in life? I don't know. We need to have certain experiences in life to trigger other experiences and memories so that we can heal. Upon reflection, everything that I have lived has been in sync with my chart and was preparation for now. Maybe knowing this information could have helped my parents to steer me along paths that were more compatible with who I came here to be and what I am here to learn. However, I think most of my experiences were (and are) necessary for me to reach my current level of awareness.

Tapping in doesn't mean that you glorify and glamorize the information in your chart. Your natal chart is meant to be used as a guide or reference point for your life. You came here with this information so that you can use it when you need clarity and to help you to remember what you are here for. You have work to do, including traumas to heal and people to help.

You may already be on mission even though you know nothing about natal charts. That's cool. This information will still be useful because you don't know what you don't know until it is revealed to you. It is also for people who are challenged to the point of stagnation. When you understand that having a natal chart means that you are not meant to struggle or have a hit-or-miss life, you develop clarity and become confident in who you are. The information you've been seeking all of your life has been available to you all along. With it at your disposal, you can have a better understanding of yourself, as well as your relationships with family members and others. You can share with family and friends who are open to receiving this knowing.

It doesn't matter that you are just learning about your natal chart as an adult. In fact, it is a bonus to receive this information later in life where you are better able to resonate with its significance and benefits. You probably already were living your life loosely based on your blueprint. You're therefore less likely to doubt what's in it. Now that your natal chart has confirmed that you are on the right track, you can continue to move forward with greater confidence and clarity.

People talk about life hacks.[27] Well, your natal chart is the ultimate life hack on your path!

You can research your natal chart at www.astro-seek.com and https://astro.cafeastrology.com. An astrologer or other counselor who specializes in astrology can help you to get a deeper understanding of what your chart means. Allow your Higher Self to guide you to healers who you can trust.

> **Be careful who you choose to consult. Avoid people who might try to exploit your naïveté by following your intuition and only connecting with whom you resonate.**

The Resources section of this Manual contains information on reputable practitioners who will not take advantage of you.

---

[27] "[A] life hack . . . is any trick, shortcut, skill, or novelty method that increases productivity and efficiency, in all walks of life." Retrieved from *Wikipedia*: https://en.m.wikipedia.org/wiki/Life_hack.

What's Next...

We will talk about the media you should be tuning into.

Chapter Nine: …And Tap in to Your "Built-in" Support Team

You know how your job or business has support staff like office managers, administrative assistants, customer service representatives, secretaries, bookkeepers, IT technicians, file clerks, copy clerks, and so on? Well, you also have support.

Nope. Not your family and friends. Not even your coworkers.

Your personal support staff is your Spirit Team. They exist on a higher dimension and volunteered to be your guides in this lifetime to help you to heal and fulfill your mission. Connecting with yourself includes consciously connecting with your Team. For me, this is a significant part of the journey to meta-Knowing and your meta-Self. This connection helps you to transcend survival mode because you connect (or reconnect) with your spiritual self. Connecting with your Team takes the guess work out of your life.

Maybe you have dreamt about, seen and/or heard things as a child (or adult) that scared you. You probably believed that what you were experiencing is evil or were called crazy if you tried to talk about it with family or friends. So, you blocked out these events until they stopped occurring. That doesn't mean that your Spirit Team is no longer with you. They are quietly waiting for you to connect with them. In the meantime, they do what they can to protect and help you along in your journey.

You know that your Spirit Team is with you when you're not consciously tapping in through events that you think of as coincidences. For instance, one evening after work, I was waiting for the train at Grand Central Station in New York. All of a sudden, I heard a voice say "move to the other car." I thought that was weird, but I obeyed. The train came and the car I entered was very crowded for after rush hour. No one was in the car that I would have entered had I ignored the voice. I knew something was wrong and I remained in the crowded car. Finally, I made it to my stop. As I walked past the empty car, a strong stench hit me. I noticed that a man was sitting in that car and had made a huge mess in it. Had I not listened to the "voice", I would have had a really traumatizing end to my work day.

I had another experience on 9/11/2001. I was running late for work as the morning's events unfolded. People around me on the train seemed to be concerned about something, but I couldn't hear what they were saying. I had no idea what was happening because I didn't have a television or cell phone. When I arrived at my stop someone asked me where I was going and had I heard about what was happening. I called the office and was told to go home. Still clueless, I did. Later on, I learned that the heavy iron light fixture that was hanging over my desk somehow fell from the ceiling around the time I would have been sitting there. Not only was I protected from having to walk across the Brooklyn Bridge in high heels to get home, but I was guided away from a life-threatening incident.

Now that you know that you're never alone and that there are actually spirits who want to help you navigate this life, it's time to develop a conscious connection with them. When you are spirit-led you no longer have to guess what moves you should make in your life because you can ask for guidance. You can easily avoid unnecessary problems. Being spirit-led helps you to achieve work-life balance and effectively manage stress.

🕊 Who is on your spirit team?

Your cultural, ethnic and/or religious background might determine who and/or what you call the members of your Spirit Team. Generally, your Spirit Team consists of:

1. Your HIGHER SELF – is your soul, or as I call it, your meta-Self. Your Higher Self knows you best having experienced many lifetimes, and has information and answers for you. Your higher self knows if it makes

47

sense for you to apply for that job at that particular company or date that particular person, and so on.

2. Your BENEVOLENT ANCESTORS KNOWN AND UNKNOWN – are the members of your team with whom you share DNA. As a beginner, connect with your benevolent ancestors because they love you unconditionally and choose to work with you for your highest and greatest good. Assume that the grandmother who disliked your mother and never had anything kind to say to you will not change after she transitions. She might guide you off a cliff.

3. Your SPIRIT GUIDES – are your team members who are not connected to you by DNA, but volunteered to be with you in this lifetime. They could be friends, former neighbors, or other people who knew you before they transitioned.

4. ASCENDED MASTERS – are people who mastered what they were supposed to do before transitioning and their mastery is now available to you. These are people like Dr. Sebi, Michael Jackson, Malcolm X, Prince and DMX.

5. THE MOST HIGH or SOURCE or GOD or THE CREATOR – or whatever name you use.

You might also have other beings on your team, and of course, you can call on angels for help.

Look at all of this help that you have!

There is no reason for you to be floundering in your life now that you know you have "people." Tap in!

You have free will. Therefore, your Spirit Team is not going to assume that you want them to step in and guide you unless you ask them to do so. You have to connect actively and consistently work on connecting. Other than The Most High, the Team members you want to connect with, at the outset, are your Higher

48

Self and your Benevolent Ancestors. Your relationship will progress from there as you learn how you receive your communications and who is on your Team.

Experiences like the one I had on the train will become common place after you cultivate a relationship with your Spirit Team by meditating to connect and showing them that you're paying attention to the prompts they're giving you by acting on them. They'll help you to steer clear of circumstances, events, people, places and things that are not a good fit for you.

It is important to trust your Spirit Team's guidance. Your Team has a bird's eye view of your life. They are able to see what's coming your way well before it's on your radar. For instance, you might be house-hunting and have two viable options. Instead of taking the chance that whichever one you choose will be the best one, you can consult with your Spirit Team. They already know which one of those houses is perfect for you, or even if you should be house-hunting.

🐦 You might be wondering, why do I want to connect with spirits?

Well, they literally have keys for you!

Through a line of over 1 million of your blood ancestors alone, you possess countless years of memories based on their experiences.[28]

Can you see that your DNA is a databank of information that can help you to overcome any circumstance and thrive beyond what your mind can conceive? You never have to want for anything because your ancestors already did it all and left you the code. You just have to figure out which key is for what. Why wouldn't you want to tap into that? All you have to do is commit to embracing the opportunity that metanoia presents so that you can meet your meta-Self.

---

[28] Kamene, Kaba Hiawatha. (2021). *Shabaka's Stone: An African Theory on the Origin and Continuing Development of the Cosmic Universe*, p. 51. Las Vegas, NV: Independently Published.

꙳ So, how do you cultivate a relationship with your Spirit
   Team?

Most important is that they are not meant to be
worshipped. They are there to help you. You are in control. Your
wish is their command.

That being said, the most basic way to tap in is by
meditating with the intention of connecting. This means no music
and mantras when you meditate. Otherwise, you won't hear the
messages they have for you or the answers to the questions you ask.
Just sit and listen. Allow your thoughts to come and go without
focusing on them or becoming frustrated. After a while, you will be
able to distinguish between when you're having a regular thought
and when information is coming through. The more you meditate,
the easier it will become.

You can also start talking (in your head) to them
throughout your day. Invite them to be with you throughout your
day and to remove challenges and obstacles from your path. You
can ask for help with making decisions that arise. Maybe you ask
to see a certain object, color or number as a signal for "yes" or "no."
For instance, let's say you're invited on a date by someone you
barely know and you want to know if it's safe. Ask for guidance.

Be consistent with your practice.

You're probably wondering if you can ask your Spirit Team
for specific help and/or things. You definitely can. You're in
charge. There's no need to beg and plead with them. You simply
tell them what you need. If you're supposed to have it at that time
or ever, it's yours as long as you're on your spiritual path.
Remember, they have the long view and know what's best for your
highest and greatest good.

꙳ And how do you show that you're paying attention to their
   responses and prompts?

Don't doubt the information you receive and do the
opposite of the guidance your Team provides. Remember that date
you were invited on? If you're prompted not to go, stay home.
Otherwise, they will take that to mean that you're not ready to

connect or that you don't need them to be active in your life. They'll still be there, but more as observers.

When you make your Spirit Team an active part of your life, it becomes less challenging because you're no longer guessing what to do and where to go. That is not to say you won't be challenged. However, your challenges are more bearable because you are guided and protected.

🕊   🕊   🕊

What's Next...

Although you can connect to your Spirit Team at anytime and anywhere, it's important to have a designated space in your home where you can sit at least once a day to connect. We'll talk about that in the next chapter.

Chapter Ten: Designate A Space for Connecting

One of the reasons why religious organizations have buildings where they invite masses of people to come and worship is because the congregation's energy collects in this space and creates a vibe that benefits the organization. The chanting, singing, praying and preaching fills the space with a vibration that, for example, moves congregants to reach into their pockets and give their money to a pastor as tithes when they have barely enough money to pay their bills.

How about you start benefiting from your energy for a change?

One of the ways that you can do this is by setting up an altar in your home. Before I continue, know that you don't have to this or any other practice we discuss if you're not led to by your Higher Self.

Remember how we talked in Chapter Nine about codes being locked in your DNA? Well, it could be that you are not led to have a physical altar or don't need one because you have unlocked that code. After all, the point of doing this work is to get to where you have such a connection with your meta-Self that you don't have to use the physical tools so much or if at all. On the other hand, if you are new to building your spiritual practice and are looking for direction, this is for you.

Having an altar in your home provides you with a designated space where you can meditate and cultivate your connection to your Spirit Team. With daily use, you fill the space with its own unique energy that makes it easier to communicate and connect with your Spirit Team.

Your altar doesn't have to be elaborate. It might look different depending on your cultural, ethnic or religious background. You don't have to go out and buy anything, and can use whatever you already have in your home. Follow your intuition as to the specific objects you place on your altar. Ask for guidance as to what to add. Your altar will evolve over time as you become more connected and your Spirt Team tells you what they want in that space.

Generally, you need a clean, flat surface made of a natural substance like wood (no metal or plastic), a clean white cloth, and items that represent the four elements – fire, water, air and earth. These elements can be represented by a tea light candle, a glass of good quality water, incense and a potted plant. You can add photographs of your benevolent ancestors if you have them.

If you're worried about what people might think of and say about you because you have an altar, you can place it in a part of your home where only you have access. However, at this stage, you really shouldn't be concerned about what anyone thinks or says. Eventually, they'll be doing the same thing when they see how you are benefitting from your work.

What's Next...

Let's get busy with the juicy stuff.

PART II: Tools and Tips

Now that you are developing the kind of mindset you need to free yourself from survival mode, you will find that you will be prompted to make assessments of and adjustments in certain areas of your life. This is because as you do this work, you begin to feel and want better for yourself.

In this section, we discuss some of the areas where you might be prompted to assess and adjust, the approaches you might want to take, and why. We also discuss tangible things, like practices, crystals, herbs and nutrition, that you can integrate into your upgraded lifestyle.

There is no need to invest in everything that's listed here. Instead, start with what you have. Then add what resonates with you or that you're prompted to get or do. Given that you are developing a relationship with yourself, you will know when (or if) you need a particular tool or practice, or have outgrown it.

Important to know is that the further you go on your spiritual path, the more you get to know yourself and unlock the information in your DNA. As this happens, you might find that you no longer have to use crystals, for instance, because an ancestor learned how to integrate what crystals do and you now have access to that information.

Please don't take this stuff (or yourself) too seriously! There is no right or wrong way. The best way is your way.

Above all, trust that you know all that you need to know, and have fun with it!

Chapter Eleven: Adjust Your Diet – Mind, Body and Soul

Let's talk about strategies for fortifying yourself against survival mode through what and how you feed your mind, body and soul. That's right, your nutrients don't only come from the food you put in your mouth. Your thoughts, the people you surround yourself with, the work you do, and so on, all play a role in your ability to fight dis-ease. When you build your resilience and develop strategies for decreasing and managing stress, you'll find that it becomes easier to handle life's curve balls whether you're dealing with a child on too much candy or an overly demanding boss or a pandemic.

Maintaining optimal physical, mental and spiritual health with nutrition that allows you to thrive is important. That way you can avoid or fight disease and heal faster if you get sick.[29] You can also withstand the physical and psychological/mental side effects of a stressful event more effectively. Proper nutrition at a wholistic level enhances your health and wellbeing because it helps your natural immunity to function at its peak and elevates your stress management skills.

Enriching your body with nutrients from nutrient-dense alkaline foods (foods which are high in pH or potential of hydrogen) and taking supplements where necessary, helps to keep you in top physical, mental, emotional and spiritual shape.

---

[29] Dunkin, MA. (2009, November 16). How to Use Your Immune System to Stay Healthy. *WebMD*. Retrieved from https://www.webmd.com/a-to-z-guides/features/how-use-your-immune-system-stay-healthy.

Potential of hydrogen (pH) is measured on a scale of 0 to 14. The higher the number above 7 on the pH scale, the more alkaline is the food. The lower the number below 7 on the pH scale, the more acidic is the food. Low pH foods like dairy, meat and processed foods, form acid in the body and cause inflammation.

Although your body is naturally alkaline in some places and acidic in others, you want to intake high pH foods to maintain your health and well-being. High pH foods are organic, non-GMO, non-hybrid fruits, vegetables, herbs, seeds and nuts.

Master teachers like Dr. Sebi[30] and Dr. Llaila Afrika[31] have as their soul's mission to teach us about the food available to us. By now, you've probably heard of or seen some iteration of Dr. Sebi's alkaline food list. Dr. Afrika has written many books on nutrition.

Why don't we want to eat low pH or acidic foods? They cause mucus to build up in your body to protect your cells against their harmful effects. Apart from causing you to become physically sick, the mucus interferes with your ability to connect with your inner guidance. It's sort of like being on a phone call where you can't hear each other because of defective or cheap earbuds. On the other hand, high pH or alkaline foods provide you with information and make it easier for you to connect.

This brings to mind the term "hangry," which is when you're so hungry for high quality food that it affects your ability to function. You become easily angered and irritated at things that don't normally move you. Then you eat and all is well with the world again. All of a sudden, you have no idea why you were so mad before. This feeling of goodwill will not last for long (or even occur) if you're satisfying your hunger with low pH foods.

It's not just about physical nutrition though.

---

[30] Dr. Sebi is the name that comes to mind for many people when the term "alkaline foods" is mentioned. A Google search will reveal many food lists based on his teachings, including this one at https://drsebiscellfood.com/pages/nutritional-guide. You can also find a food list and recipes at www.tysconsciouskitchen.com.

[31] Dr. Llaila Afrika wrote several books on nutrition, a few of which are listed in the Bibliography in this Manual.

You can be eating high pH foods and working out every day, but still feel crappy because of what and who you allow into your life and mind, or your living environment. When you eat high pH foods and can surround yourself with people, places and things, who help you to become and feel better, whether they know it or not, your body becomes a clear(er) channel. It becomes easier to determine what and who needs to be removed from your life so that survival mode is a thing of the past for you.

The clearer you become the better you will be able intuitively to know how to respond to your circumstances and environment in a way that benefits you. You will know what practices you will benefit from the most in your daily routine. You'll be better able to articulate your needs and desires so that you get exactly what you need.

Please note that none of the above means that you should deprive yourself of fun and flavor. And never beat yourself up for indulging in food that's not considered to be alkaline. Ultimately, this is all a mind game.

The Basics

At the very least:

- Intake organic, alkaline (high pH), plant-based, non-hybrid, non-GMO, unprocessed fruit, leafy green vegetables, herbs, nuts and seeds.

- Prepare your own food.

- Eat fresh fruits and vegetables.

- Use good quality dried or fresh herbs.

- Reduce/eliminate foods and supplements that contain gluten, corn, sugar, caffeine, dairy and soy.

- Reduce/eliminate the recreational use of mind-altering substances.

- Use healthy fats like non-GMO and organic olive oil (make sure it's not diluted with soybean oil), avocado oil, sunflower seed oil, safflower oil, grapeseed oil, flax seed oil, hemp seed oil, coconut oil and fish/cod liver oil. Some of these oils should not be heated.[32]

- Exercise or engage in some type of daily physical activity that elevates your heart rate.

- Get good quality sleep.

- Take high quality dietary supplements, if necessary.

- Stay away from people and activities that deplete your energy.

---

[32] Avocado, sunflower seed and safflower oils are probably the only ones on this list that can be heated for cooking.

- 🕊 Meditate to connect, and engage in other daily practices that calm, relax and help you to vibrate high.

- 🕊 Hydrate, hydrate, hydrate with good quality water like spring water or supercharged water. We will talk more about this in the next Chapter.

- 🕊 Learn something new and/or useful, especially if you've always wanted to know about it.

- 🕊 Do something creative even if it's one of those adults' (or children's) coloring books, or play with a child.

- 🕊 Go outside and get some sun.

Some Specifics

Now, let's talk about the other types of nutrition that are important for your health and wellness.

1. Nutrition and Exercise

When you're in survival mode, you might cope by binge-watching television, eating junk food, and indulging in other activities that don't serve you. This can send an internal signal that you don't care about your health. When unexpected events like the 2020 lockdown happen, some or all of these activities might become your go-to even if you had been fairly mindful about your intake and activities before. Before you know it, you've packed on weight and developed health issues that you never anticipated.

In the beginning of the pandemic, you probably thought that the restrictions would end in a few weeks, if so long. When that proved to be wrong, you probably soon started to notice the side effects of too much sitting around. Only sweat pants felt comfortable. Then your stomach always felt full so that undigested food piled up and caused your upper abdomen to have a bulge when you sit. Even though you might not have been eating more than before, you were not as active and your digestion had slowed down. It happened to me.

It's not too late to make adjustments in how you're eating and regain some sense of balance and control. You can start by having a lighter breakfast later in the morning, setting a deadline for your last meal of the day and sticking to it, adding high pH foods and reducing your intake of low pH foods, drinking more good quality water, and starting a home exercise program using moves you know or following along to YouTube videos. Do what resonates with you. It might take some time, but consistency is key.

You should already be building a relationship with yourself and should be more in tune with your body. So, set the intention to provide your body with what it needs to maintain your health and resilience, introduce whatever you need to stay motivated, and be consistent. Eventually, you will start to see and feel the results of your hard work.

If you're a woman, you've probably noticed that stress and low pH foods (which add more stress) aggravate issues that menstruating and menopausal women can face. Reportedly, increased stress can affect a woman's heart, immune response, concentration, mental and emotional health, sleep, skin and menstrual patterns.[33] Maybe your cycle is heavy with severe cramps and lasts 7 or more days every month or you feel fatigued all of the time or you have severe menopausal symptoms. These could be symptoms of other issues with your body that are beyond the scope of this book. However, making adjustments in the food you eat, and the cosmetic and household products you use, as well as your mindset, can help you to reduce your symptoms.

Women, and men, can eliminate or reduce foods and products containing gluten, corn, sugar, alcohol, caffeine, dairy, soy, and toxic chemicals. Read package labels for any and every thing you plan on intaking to make sure you're not taking in harmful substances. Reconsider products whose labels contain more than 5 ingredients or ingredients whose names you can't pronounce.

If you have chronic physical symptoms that nothing seems to heal, you can do an elimination diet. Discontinue for one month your intake of food and products containing any or all of the above substances. If your symptoms subside, add them back in one by one (a week at a time) to see if any symptoms return. If so, you should stop using that substance or product.

You also can fast (with supervision if you're new to the process) to reset your body. Just know that returning to your old lifestyle post-fast will eliminate the benefits of the fast. You therefore have to be ready to make changes in your life.

---

[33] Kittredge, C. (2017, December 14). The Physical Side of Stress: Frazzled by Stress? Learn how it affects your emotional and physical health – and how to cope. *Everyday Health*. Retrieved from www.everydayhealth.com/womens-health/physical-side-of-stress.aspx.

Of course, everything does not work for everyone. This is why you have to experiment on yourself to see what works for you. I guarantee, though, that if you take the steps to upgrade your diet and add in some exercise, you will see a huge improvement in your health and well-being. You could save yourself a lot of money in the long-run.

2. <u>Hydration</u>

Proper hydration is key to proper nutrition, and maintaining your health and wellness. Just as you cannot effectively manage stress on a low pH diet, you cannot effectively manage stress if you're constantly dehydrated. Dehydration causes you to feel irritable, dizzy, headachy, crave low pH foods, and to be unable to function properly.[34]

There might be times when you think you're hungry, but you're really dehydrated. When you feel hungry even though you've recently eaten, drink some water first to make sure that you're not actually thirsty.

Among other things, adequate hydration helps your muscles to function and to oxygenate your entire body, protects and lubricates your brain and joints, improves your immune system, digestion and mood, helps with weight loss, keeps your skin and mucus membranes moist, and helps you to sweat to maintain a healthy body temperature during exercise.[35] [36] [37]

------

[34] George, Nancie. (2020, Oct. 5). 6 Unusual Signs of Dehydration You Should Know About. *Everyday Health*. Retrieved from www.everydayhealth.com/news/unusual-signs-of-dehydration/.

[35] Ching, Julie MS, RDN, CDE. (2013, April 11). Benefits of Staying Hydrated. *Active Beat*. Retrieved from www.activebeat.com/diet-nutrition/10-benefits-of-staying-hydrated/10/.

[36] McIntosh, James. (2018, July 16). Fifteen Benefits of Drinking Water. *Medical News Today*. Retrieved from www.medicalnewstoday.com/articles/290814.

[37] Water Science School. (2019, May 22). The Water in You: Water and the Human Body. *USGS*. Retrieved from www.usgs.gov/special-topics/water-science-school/science/water-you-water-and-human-body#overview.

Your body is made up of approximately 70% fluids. The basic recommendation for daily intake is at least eight 16-ounce glasses of water. You can keep a water bottle within your reach at all times to ensure that you meet the daily requirement.

Here's the thing, you can be dehydrated even though you drink a gallon of water a day. This is because bottled water might be treated to remove or add substances and to artificially alkalinize it. It's best to drink spring water or water that you have purified yourself. To enhance the quality of your drinking water so that your cells easily absorb the water you can infuse your water with lime juice, cucumber, watermelon or other fruit. You also can eat the fruit and drink herbal teas.

Certain crystals and metals can also improve the quality of your drinking and cooking water. Quartz crystals – amethyst, clear quartz, rose quartz – are great tools for improving the structure of water. Shungite crystals not only improve your water's structure, but detox and purify water from questionable sources. Finally, storing water in and drinking water from copper vessels has many benefits, including killing any harmful bacteria in your water.

There are many tools and devices of varied prices that are available for improving the quality of the water that is available to us. In Chapter Twelve, we will discuss a simple way to hydrogenate your drinking water so that it is more beneficial for your body.

3. Education

A lot of the stress in your life could be coming from not having access to what you need to overcome the challenges you face. This will change as you begin to know yourself better.

While formal education (hopefully) teaches you how to read, write and add, it doesn't equip you with the ability to remember who you truly are. Formal education is designed to take your focus away from knowing yourself to knowing how to be the best employee you can be. You learn to concentrate on earning money to buy things, while trusting your health and well-being to those who do not have your best interests at heart. You are educated to rely on modalities outside of yourself to tell you who you are. In this sense, formal education is a dumbing down.

You already have the information in your DNA that you need to thrive in this life. To the extent that you recall some of those things early on, formal education causes you to distrust that you know what you need and how to recognize when you're being guided by your inner knowing.

It's like handling a legal case. There might be factual nuances in the case that the usual rules don't quite fit. Instead of assuming that she will lose the case, however, the lawyer will do research to find different rules that fit or ways to apply the old rules so that they work for her client. Well, this technique applies to your personal life. However, when you know yourself, you don't have to do any research outside of yourself. You will find that a challenge arises and you immediately know what to do even though you might dismiss it and try other things before realizing that the very first thing you thought of will resolve your issue. When you know yourself, you can trust that your knowing is more valuable than anything you can learn in a school or from anyone else.

Now, sometimes, as with the pandemic, the external information can be scary and confusing so that you doubt your inner knowing. Instead of constantly following what confuses and alarms you, you can educate yourself on how best to protect yourself from whatever the media is pushing as the latest crisis.

The bottom line is that the type of education that truly helps to decrease your stress levels and improve your health and well-being does not necessarily come from formal education. Approach your life with this in mind and you'll be less likely to be constantly fearful and confused, and more likely to believe that only you know what's best for you.

4. <u>Spiritual/Religious Practices</u>

Don't allow the chaos around you to prevent you from using the spiritual and religious tools and practices that have always worked for you. Whatever you used to do to keep yourself sane before chaos ensued is valuable if it worked. You should definitely continue with it.

Just because your regular place of worship might be closed because of a pandemic doesn't mean that you have no options. You don't need a pastor to tell you how to tap in. Your temple is wherever you are.[38]

If you did nothing pre-chaos because you couldn't find a place for it in your busy life, adding things like daily prayer and meditation to your routine can be comforting when life seems to be taking a turn for the worse. A routine will help you to stay centered, grounded and de-stressed (not distressed).

Maybe every morning when you rise you can say a prayer or recite your favorite Psalm or simply give thanks for your many blessings. You also can meditate. You can designate a specific area in your home that you go to everyday for this practice, if that helps you to be consistent.

We'll talk more about meditation in the next Chapter.

5. <u>Job/Career</u>

When life is upended, you might be triggered to assess whether your job/career is truly serving your best interests. If work is challenging, the extra load of a pandemic, for instance, can be a breaking point. You may not want to or be able to leave your job. But you might think about what's not working and address that. Maybe you can negotiate with your boss for better working conditions or pay. Or maybe you can turn into a lucrative business that passion for making jewelry that you set aside because of the demands of your job. Not only could this turn out to be a source of

---

[38] 1 Corinthians 6:19-20.

income that allows you to leave your job behind, but it could be the perfect way to de-compress daily from the chaos.

At the very least, focusing on your passion means you're spending more time on self-improvement and less time watching the news, shows and movies that are designed to be constant reminders of depressing events, and to distract you. Even if you continue to tune into CNN and them, it will probably be more entertaining than stressful because you are working on yourself and know what's true for you.

From all indications, many Americans made this type of assessment and chose not to return to work, creating a huge staffing shortage in just about every industry. They call it "the Great Resignation."[39]

If you are prompted to assess your life, it does not necessarily mean that you have to quit your job. This is why knowing yourself is important. When you are faced with questions like this, you can tap into your Higher Self for your answers.

6. Work-Life Balance

I think we need to touch on work-life balance, which is an important topic for many, especially women in the work place.

In my opinion, work-life balance is unattainable as long as you're working in the human-as-capital paradigm. You're working in a system which needs you to be unbalanced and always in survival mode because the system cannot survive otherwise. The most you can do is to rely on your proverbial "village" for help. Career women of means who have children hire nannies and housekeepers to help them to care for their families while they work. Other women manage as best as they can with the help of available family and friends. Still others do the best they can. Regardless, they all make sacrifices and endure stress.

---

[39] Chugh, Abhinav. (2021, Nov 29). What is 'The Great Resignation'? An expert explains. *World Economic Forum*. Retrieved from www.weforum.org/agenda/2021/11/what-is-the-great-resignation-and-what-can-we-learn-from-it/

True work-life balance comes from being in alignment with your soul's mission and doing the work that you signed up for in this lifetime. Doing this work doesn't mean that you have to be poor or a monk/nun. You are more likely to manifest a consistent source of income and a life of ease when you're pursuing your mission.

Your work is not in alignment with your mission if you constantly feel as if something is not right with how you're making a living. You might be making a substantial amount of money annually, but your lifestyle is detrimental to your mind, body and spirit. And you know it. That's your intuition clueing you in. You have to figure out what you are here to do, unless you already know and are ignoring your calling.

You find balance on your spiritual path by working on your mission because this is the work you came here to do. Spirit wants you to complete that task. So, you'll receive the balance you need to get it done provided that you're actively pursuing it.

7. Relationships & Social Life

Humans are social beings. Introvert or extrovert, we thrive on social connections.[40] Social distancing is an oxymoron; a sick joke.

Pre-pandemic, we all took for granted the freedom we had to socialize with whomever and whenever. Having meaningful relationships with others boosts your mental health, extends your life span, decreases your risk for suicide, and helps you to have an

---

[40] According to the CDC, surveys conducted in the US in late June 2020 showed that "40% of U.S. adults reported struggling with mental health or substance use" due to the pandemic. Not only did people report mental health or behavioral conditions and disorders, but they reported starting, or increasing substance use to cope with the pandemic. Czeisler M., Lane R.I., Petrosky E., et al. Mental Health Substance Use, and Suicidal Ideation During COVID-19 Pandemic – United States, June 24-30, 2020, MMWR Morb Mortal Wkly Rep 2020; 69:1049-1057. DOI: http://dx.doi.org/10.15585/mmwr.mm6932a1. Retrieved from www.cdc.gov/mmwr/volumes/69/wr/mm6932a1.htm.

appearance of work-life balance, among other things.[41] The opposite happens when we cannot connect with each other.

When we can no longer access our environment in the ways we want to it creates stress. I would venture to say that it breaks our hearts because the source of our connection (our toroidal field or aura) emanates from our heart.[42]

There's a huge difference between choosing to be alone and loneliness. When you're involuntarily isolated, it can bring on loneliness because you're prevented from acting on your instinct to be with other people. This can lead to mental health problems depending on the length of time that you're isolated, your personality, and other variables.[43]

The forced separation and isolation associated with the 2020 pandemic had mental, physical and spiritual side effects. Reportedly, being in circumstances with no end in sight and the inability to give and receive in-person support to and from your loved ones added to the anxiety and depression many experienced during and since the pandemic. [44]

Doesn't that sound like it is heart-related?

When the world shuts down because of an isolating pandemic, how do you cope when the only way you can connect with loved ones is through electronic devices? What do you do when you can't just hop on a plane and go on a vacation or to visit family and friends to decompress? What if you live alone and/or in a city where you have no relatives and no real friends? Even worse,

---

[41] Id.

[42] Ledwell, Natalie. (February 10, 2020). Toroidal Energetic Field? What Tha?! *Mind Movies*. Retrieved from www.mindmovies.com/blogroll/toroidal-energetic-field-what-tha.

[43] Chadra, Anshdeep Singh. (August 14, 2020). The Importance of Human Connections. *The Pangean*. Retrieved from thepangean.com/The-Importance-of-Human-Connections.

[44] The Importance of Social Connection. *Mindwise Innovation*. Retrieved from www.mindwise.org/blog/uncategorized/the-importance-of-social-connection/.

what if you are forced to lockdown with an abuser and no longer have access to the few hours at work or school that separated you from them?

It's not that we didn't use electronic devices to connect pre-pandemic. We took for granted that we'd always be able to have personal contact with our loved ones at our leisure. The devices were for communicating in between meet-ups and for arranging for meet-ups. Suddenly these devices are the only means for seeing and speaking with our loved ones. Zoom parties and weddings have become the norm.

While some restrictions have been lifted, some people are still isolated and/or prefer to isolate themselves out of fear of getting sick. Some people are even ostracizing family and friends because of their opinions on current events and treatment.

Relationships are necessary for learning the lessons that we need to evolve and elevate our consciousness.[45] If you're isolated from everyone, you cannot make the kinds of connections you need to grow and heal.[46]

On the other hand, if you're living in close quarters with people during stressful times, there's likely to be friction. "Violence against women and girls, particularly domestic violence, has intensified" since the pandemic started.[47] This spike in violence is probably not limited to women and girls. Rather than being abusive, it would be more beneficial for abusers to do the work on

---

[45] The Various Kinds of Spiritual Relationships That Can Exist in Your Life. *Aristos Lifestyle*. Retrieved from www.aristoslifestyle.com/articles/the-different-kinds-of-spiritual-relationships.

[46] Id.

[47] The Shadow Pandemic: Violence Against Women During COVID-19. *UN Women*. Retrieved from www.unwomen.org/en/news/in-focus-gender-equality-in-covid-19-response/violence-against-women-during-covid-19.

themselves to learn what their relationships are supposed to teach them.[48]

Unfortunately, I don't think anyone has clear answers on how to deal with forced and enforced isolation, although you can resist and do you. This is why it is important to go inward and connect with yourself so that you remember what works for you.

Some things you can do are:

- Find uplifting and creative ways to sustain your relationships with loved ones and to make healthy, new connections.

- Take responsibility for yourself.

- Take a walk to clear your head when you feel like lashing out.

- Don't "disown" a good friend just because they don't share your views on how to handle current events. Agree to disagree and talk about something else.

- Sign up for a live class on a topic that interests you.

- Stop believing that controlling someone else is helping you.

8. Home Environment

Want to add stress to stress? Keep a cluttered and messy home or work environment – physically and mentally. You have to

---

[48] The Various Kinds of Spiritual Relationships That Can Exist in Your Life. *Aristos Lifestyle*. Retrieved from www.aristoslifestyle.com/articles/the-different-kinds-of-spiritual-relationships

declutter your physical spaces and your mind to open up room for what you truly want and need.

A. Physical Decluttering

Cleaning a messy home helps you to ease your stress levels. If you are generally a tidy person, tending to neglected areas of your home, like closets and drawers, and clearing out hidden clutter can be helpful. The process of cleaning helps you to de-stress. Plus seeing all of that empty space gives you a sense of accomplishment and raises your spirits.

If you previously did a deep clean once a month because you spent a lot of time at the office, now you can clean twice a month or weekly. Things you use every day can be cleaned and freshened as you go. With sparkling floors and appliances, orderly closets and drawers, and all of the dishes washed in a timely manner, you have less distractions.

You can make decluttering a family occasion. Or if you live alone, you can take a room per day. If you weren't taught how to clean, there are many YouTube videos on how to do various household chores. Play your favorite music as you clean or make it a time for quiet reflection.

If you have decided to leave your job and pursue your soul's mission, you can probably donate your clothing and shoes that no longer fit your lifestyle. Giving away and/or selling gently used clothing and jewelry you haven't worn in a long time, especially if you plan not to return to your pre-pandemic lifestyle, is a great idea.

B. Psychic Decluttering

Another way to declutter your space, especially if you share it with others, is to work on yourself instead of blaming others for your discomfort. We've all sustained traumas, especially as children, that follow us into adulthood. These traumas drive the destructive things we say, feel and think about that we discussed in Chapter Three. When you're triggered, it's time to heal the trauma that's coming up by doing chakra healing work.

Ever been bullied or teased by schoolmates or siblings? Or maybe you were abused as a child or witnessed a sibling or another child being abused. These things stay with us even though we may not remember specifics or believe they had an effect.

These are the underlying events that trigger us to react strongly or violently if someone makes a comment or does something that wouldn't be an issue under other circumstances. For instance, you might ask someone a question that evokes a response that triggers an unwarranted reaction from you, not realizing that your issue with their response stems from a traumatic event in your childhood.

You experience traumas in your early life that can cause you to lose balance and focus in your lives. Where you were once confident in who you are, you start to doubt yourself and/or hide a part of yourself to avoid attention or being hurt. Eventually, you're holding that aspect is so deep that you forget it happened and that it relates to your current way of being.

This imbalance shows up in different ways in your life and your relationships, and definitely lodges in your body's energy centers or chakras, depending on the trauma.[49] Your experiences (good and bad) are essentially stored in your chakras as energy. The bad experiences or traumas can prevent you from making true progress in your life. You may have the best job, a mansion on a hill and luxury cars, but be completely miserable. In your misery, you're probably reactive, sometimes violently, to those around you because their actions trigger you.

Well, instead of lashing out at yourself (through your thoughts and beliefs), and your relatives and friends or who/whatever is your trigger, you have to go inward and examine why you're so bothered. This is the time to ask yourself questions about why you are triggered. Make a conscious effort to meditate on your questions and ask for answers. Trust that whatever comes to mind is the truth. From there you can work on transmuting that

---

[49] Anthony, K. (2020). *Chakra Nova: You Are the Book*. Middletown, DE: https://columbianxchange.com/products/chakra-nova.

trauma so that it no longer runs your life, unless you enjoy playing the victim.

Transmuting trauma can mean having a conversation with a parent or guardian who convinced you that you'll never amount to anything, for instance, to tell them how it made you feel and how it affected your life. That conversation could help to open up space in your life for things to start to flow financially and creatively where there was once stagnation. In this way, you heal your chakras so that you escape from survival mode.

You might also consider working with a counselor or coach who can provide simple tips and recommendations that you might not have considered for clearing the residue of your trauma. Counseling can be beneficial if a conversation with your "traumatizer" is insufficient or not possible, and/or if the trauma is severe like child sexual abuse or domestic violence. However, with counseling you still have to do your own work.

Ultimately, de-cluttering brings joy, peace, harmony, clarity, and so much more. It allows you to truly focus on being productive and creative because it opens up space in your mind, body and spirit that was occupied by what you didn't want.

9. <u>Finances</u>

Being in a financial position where you never have to worry about how you'll pay for your necessities and pleasures is the ultimate dream. A huge area of stress for many of us is how to have sufficient money to achieve this dream. There's always a bill to be paid. It seems like only a small percentage of the world's population never have to think/worry about having enough. The rest of us are in survival mode working hard to pay bills and buy things.

One of the first things I learned in high school Economics is the carrot and stick theory. As I was taught, this theory comes from the fact that if you want a stubborn donkey to work really hard for you, dangle a carrot on a stick just far enough away from its mouth that the donkey is so focused on getting to the carrot that it doesn't realize it is doing the hard work.

Most of us are the donkeys who work really hard for a fraction of what we generate so that the rest never have to worry about how they will pay their bills for generations to come.

When you think about it, our way of life really makes no sense. We are indoctrinated, from the time we're born, to believe that we are supposed to work hard to earn an income to buy even the simplest pleasures of life and for essentials like housing, clothing, food and water. We are led to believe that if we follow the rules and work hard enough, we will retire to live our best life with a huge stash of retirement cash.

Maybe as a youth just out of high school, the prospect of getting a job/career and making money is appealing. However, the longer you're in this system, the more resistant to it you become. Your resistance first shows up in physical, mental and spiritual discomfort. Most cannot define what's happening because they are in survival mode, which leaves no room for taking stock of your life.

You're working so hard that it never occurs to you to question your lifestyle. You're always chasing the carrot because you are not meant to get it. The piece of it that you receive in a paycheck is often never ever enough to fulfill your needs, much less your wants. It's just enough to keep you coming back with the promise of raises and bonuses to push you a little closer to that small percentage of people we talked about.

The real carrot and stick work allows you to have true, lasting freedom from worrying about finances. When you choose to pursue your true purpose, the "stick" is that if you consistently tune into and heed your inner guidance, you will be rewarded with the "carrot," i.e., your needs will always be taken care of beyond what your mind can conceive and your desires can be easily obtained. In other words, figure out what you're here to do, do that consistently, and allow your inner guidance to be your boss in order to shift from surviving to thriving. Life gradually becomes easier and less stressful, and you no longer have to worry about how to clothe, feed and house yourself and your family.

By being consistent on your path, you learn lessons and earn blessings/blissings. The carrot (rewards from being on your path) show up with little effort. Now you're thriving.

On your path, you learn to follow your intuition. You are guided to use your innate gifts and talents to ease your financial stress. This doesn't mean that there won't be challenges. However, things will always work out for your benefit if you stay on course.

10. <u>Don't Be Afraid to Ask for Help</u>

You're not meant to do everything alone or figure out from scratch processes that have already been done, i.e., reinvent the wheel. It is not humiliating to ask for and/or to need help. You don't know what you don't know that can improve your chances of thriving. More than likely, you know someone (or they know someone) who had the same experiences you're having and can offer you their wisdom.

You know how sometimes you're drawn to a stranger (or vice versa) who might be on a checkout line with you and you speak up? You might start off talking about how slowly the line is moving. Then the next thing you know that stranger has uploaded into you the solution for a problem you faced with no idea that you were looking for those answers. It could be as simple as that.

Sometimes you need to consult with an expert on the issue you are facing. Be prepared for the possibility that they might charge you a fee. If their fee is not in your budget, move on and keep looking for someone who can help you. Don't be verbally abusive.

Do not expect people to give away their innate gifts, talents and abilities for free. It's hard enough for some to become comfortable with charging a fee for doing what they love and to develop the courage to ask for one.

> **Know that it's a currency exchange that benefits you, as well. It's all energy. You get back what you put out.**

Whatever you do – a conversation with family/friends/a stranger or an expert – make your life easier by asking for help. It makes no sense to get stuck in the limiting belief that you have to do it all yourself. This is simply not true.

Ultimately, you want to be so connected with yourself that your answers come from within. Either you get the answer from your Higher Self, or you are led to the people who can help you (like the stranger on the checkout line).

11. <u>Go Outside</u>

It is imperative to go outside and enjoy nature. Sun and greenspace exposure is very beneficial for your health and wellbeing. Similarly, a visit to a river or ocean is highly recommended.

It has been known since at least 1968 that visible and near infrared waves from the sun promote healing.[50] Specifically, early morning and late afternoon sun exposure can prevent health issues and repair the body.[51]

Exposure to greenspaces also promotes improved pregnancy outcomes, and reduced diastolic blood pressure, heart rate, salivary

---

[50] Barolet, D, et al. (2016). Infrared and skin: Friend or foe. Journal of Photochemistry & Photobiology, B: Biology 155 (2016 78-85, 81.

[51] <u>Id</u>., 84.

cortisol, type II diabetes and strokes, and death from heart disease.[52]

12. Don't Discount the Wisdom of Your Elders

Following from the notion that you can and should ask for help when you need it, you can reach out to your elders for their wisdom. You've probably heard that "there is nothing new under the sun."[53] Who knows this better than your elders?

They have experienced a lifetime, which exposed them to many of the experiences you're having. A lot of the time they're seeing you going through it and have guidance to offer. They can give you strategies and recommendations for preventing, avoiding and navigating your challenges. But you never ask. You probably ignore and/or reject them because they are older and grew up in different times.

You live in an era where life seems far removed from the life your elders led when they were your age. Now, everything seems to move faster, technology is relatively more advanced, and social media is a thing. But at their core, the challenges the younger generations face are essentially the same. A conversation with an elder about how they feel about the way they lived their life and their biggest regrets could be an eye-opening experience for you. You can gain valuable insight on how to avoid similar regrets that you anticipate are looming in your future. Although the technology is different, the basics of how to be in a relationship with a spouse remain the same.

Most likely grandma and grandpa spent a lot of time chasing the next new thing, working long hours, and blaming others for their choices, instead of working on themselves and taking responsibility for their lives. They didn't know better at the

---

[52] Twohig-Bennett, Coainhe, et al. (2018). The health benefits of the great outdoors: A systematic review and meta-analysis of greenspace exposure and health outcomes. Environmental Research 166 (2018) 628-637, 636.

[53] Ecclesiastes 1:9.

time. But they now know what they would/should have done differently. That's valuable information for you. You can save yourself a lot of trouble and time by listening to them talk about their lives.

A conversation with an elder can give you the kind of perspective the Law of Relativity implies. You might learn that your life really isn't as bad as you think and that there's always a solution to whatever challenge you're facing.

Connecting with an elder, especially those among your blood relatives like your parents and grandparents and the people who knew/know them intimately also can help you to understand these people in a way that opens your heart to them and helps you to heal from childhood traumas they might have inflicted knowingly or unknowingly.

Hear me out. Most parents, at least the ones from my generation, don't tell us about the upbringing and experiences that influenced how and why they raised us the way they did. Whether you were raised by both parents or neither, learning your caregiver's story can help you to understand why they took certain actions and said certain things, or didn't.

Say, for instance, you were raised by a single mother and your father never showed up when he said he would. Your mother doesn't necessarily know his story beyond what she experienced of him. So, outside of your own thoughts and feelings about his absence, you are also subjected to hers through the thoughts, feeling and words she projects to you about him. Over time, you can't help but develop a certain attitude toward your father even though you haven't heard his side of the story.

Another scenario is that you might have been raised in a two-parent household with a strict father. Going to parties with your friends or having a boyfriend as a teenaged girl may have been taboo, and you resent your father. On top of that you might have been beaten, or observed your siblings being beaten, for breaking rules or doing things that, in hindsight, a child shouldn't be punished that severely for, if at all.

In both of these scenarios you experienced traumatic childhood events. You now resent and dislike your parent(s) and are unable to connect meaningfully with them. This affects your ability to connect meaningfully with others. That is, until one day you learn things about your parents that sheds light on their why. One little story about how their parents raised them lifts the cloud of resentment and dislike from you and humanizes them. Not only that. You are now available for the goodness of life that you were missing out on while under that cloud, and it shows in how smoothly your life is suddenly flowing.

So, connect with your elders and pick their brains!

13. You Run Things, Not "the Man!"

One of the things you might do sometimes is talk about how all of your challenges in life are caused by an unknown entity identified as "the Man" who runs things, and that there's nothing you can do to change your circumstances. You might blame "the Man" for everything from being stuck in a dead-end job to the world's events.

The thing is that "the Man" is a trick to keep you chasing the wrong carrot. "His" role is to keep you from understanding that you create your reality. "The Man" cannot exist without your focus and belief that "he's" a factor! As long as you have someone to blame for what you think is happening to you, you'll stay stuck in survival mode. The solution is to forget about "the Man," understand that you create your reality, and focus on remembering how to thrive.

The words you use, the thoughts you think, the attitudes you project, all contribute to how your life progresses. You do it consciously and subconsciously. A simple example of consciously is when your work calendar is filled with back-to-back assignments and you're so exhausted that you wish the next thing would be postponed or cancelled, and it is.

How many good things have you willed into non-existence because you subconsciously believe you cannot or should not have them because "the Man" is in control?

The bottom line is that even if "the Man" exists, he has no control over you unless you accept that "he" does. Again, it's all a mind game.

🕊   🕊   🕊

What's Next...

Challenging times affect every aspect of our lives. On the other hand, challenges present us with opportunities to upgrade ourselves, and therefore our lives, in ways that make it easier for us to withstand those challenges.

In the next chapter we will discuss a few specific tools, including mindfulness practices, supplements and herbs, that are beneficial for the upgrading process.

Chapter Twelve: Practical Tools and Tips

As you work on knowing yourself, you'll learn about physical tools and practices that are helpful for your journey. The information can be overwhelming if you're not sure how to start and what to do. The trick is to start with whatever resonates with you. That alone will bring to you what you need.

In this chapter, we will discuss some of the basic tools and practices that you can experiment with. This information is designed to give you a start and an idea of what you're working with. At some point your inner guidance will kick in and guide you to what is best for you and what you no longer need.

We will start with the practical, and then we'll talk about dietary supplements, herbs, essential oils, sacred plants, and crystals.

Mindfulness Practices

Yoga means union or communion. The goal of yoga is to unite your physical, mental and spiritual selves through being mindful of how you connect with yourself and others (yama and niyama), movement (asanas or the poses), breathwork (pranayama), and focusing inward at deepening levels (pratyahara and dhyrana) until you get to meditation (dhyana), in order to achieve a state of bliss or peace known as samadhi.[54]

Samadhi doesn't mean that nothing ever bothers you again. It means that life's curve balls no longer affect you as drastically as before. You are in a state where you are less likely to be reactive and more likely to effortlessly overcome challenges. It's easier to navigate your life when you're at peace and/or you can find peace in the midst of chaos. You don't have to isolate yourself on a mountain top or be able to twist your body into extreme poses to achieve samadhi.

Apart from improving your flexibility and balance, yoga is centering and grounding. Its many benefits include improved immunity, mental and emotional health and stress reduction, which I can confirm.

There are many apps and online resources available for starting a home yoga practice. Practitioners regularly post on YouTube and Instagram instructional videos that cater to all levels of expertise. Videos where the yogi talks you through the poses and caters for your level of flexibility in their instruction are the best.

---

[54] Iyengar, B.K.S. (1988). *The Tree of Yoga*. Shambala Classics.

Meditation. There are many ways to meditate.[55] For instance, you can do a guided meditation to music or mantras. You also can find stillness in doing your household chores, walking, exercising, and just about any activity. Some people meditate to certain sound frequencies to calm and heal themselves. However, the best sound you can meditate to is your own voice speaking affirmations and mantras to you.

The other type of meditation is to connect to yourself. When you are working on knowing yourself deeply, you want to find stillness so that you can hear your inner voice. This means sitting or lying quietly for a set period of time with your eyes closed while observing your breath and allowing your mind to wander without trying to control where it goes. No music. No mantras or affirmations. After a while, you will start to hear sounds and/or feel sensations. Make a note of these occurrences and you will notice a pattern, answers to questions you have asked, instructions, and so on.

Meditation has similar benefits to yoga that I can confirm, including stress reduction, improvement in mental and emotional health, increased mindfulness, and improved sleep.

How do you know if it's working for you? You'll notice positive changes in yourself and your environment. You'll find that your people and your environment appear to shift for the better. What is really happening is that you're shifting (or upgrading) and that's being reflected back to you.

You will benefit from meditation even if you're unable to meditate every day or only have five minutes a day. In the beginning of my practice, I meditated probably four times a year. Yet, my whole outlook changed for the better.

---

[55] Bertone, Holly J. (2020, October 2). Which Type of Meditation is Right for Me? *Healthline*. Retrieved from www.healthline.com/health/mental-health/types-of-meditation.

Breathwork (or pranayama) is the expansion of the life force within you using your breath.

You shouldn't attempt new breathing techniques for the first time without proper supervision, especially if you were diagnosed with a respiratory condition.

Learning how to breathe properly can help you to ease stress so that you thrive despite the chaos in your environment. Incorporating proper breathing techniques can help you to remain calm and relaxed if someone is trying to draw you into an argument that doesn't serve your best interest.

Mindful breathing is important for all of our daily activities.[56] The way you breathe can help or hinder you. For instance, when you hold your breath on exertion during exercise your body tenses up making it more difficult for you to move your body in the way that you want. You therefore won't be able to lift that 20-pound dumb bell as easily. Or you won't be able to twist your body into the pretzel pose you're trying to accomplish in yoga.

Sometimes you may have really tense, stressful moments where you find yourself holding your breath or breathing shallowly. This can happen when you're feeling anxiety, fear, doubt, and other lower emotions. It is difficult to be relaxed and mindful at those times. Focused breathing can be helpful.

For starters, you can practice deep breathing into your belly so that your diaphragm expands like a baby's. Diaphragmatic breathing becomes second nature the more you practice. You will quickly get to the stage where you notice when your breathing is off and can instantly make adjustments.

A useful technique that can help to release stress in the moment is to inhale for 7 counts, hold the breath for 7 counts, and

---

[56] Linda Star Wolf. (1991). *Shamanic Breathwork: Journeying Beyond the Limits of the Self.* Vermont: Bear & Company.

exhale for 7 counts. You can do this while walking, sitting, standing or lying down. After 5 or 6 repetitions, you should be in a better frame of mind to deal with whatever is bothering you.

Spiritual and Religious Practices should not be overlooked for dealing with stress. Even if you cannot get to your regular place of worship, you can still connect in your home.

A more detailed discussion on this topic is in the previous Chapter.

Reading as a means of "escaping" for a while your circumstances or to gain perspective on those circumstances should not be underestimated. You are just as likely to find clarity in a novel as you might in a religious text or a self-improvement book. So, don't judge what is available to you.

Among other things, reading can actually reduce stress, help you to understand yourself better, and reveal solutions to your challenges. You can improve your mood with a book that's quite comedic or one that takes you on an adventure. These are all good reasons for opening a book, whether it is a hard copy or on your favorite reading app.

Sound Healing/Music Therapy can help you to release stress and improve your mood and heal physical dis-ease. The sound can come from a voice, conventional musical instruments, and instruments like singing bowls and tuning forks.

Notably, musical tones or frequencies can be healing or harmful to the body, mind and spirit. At some point in the world's history, 440 hertz became the universally accepted tone for the music that is produced and commercially distributed to the population.[57] The 440 hertz frequency promotes low vibrational moods and behaviors that produce emotional distress.[58] Therefore, you could be feeling sick or depressed because of the type of music you enjoy.

While not all musicians subscribe to this 440 hertz formula, your favorite rap or pop artist could be contributing to your feelings of despair and dis-ease through the beats and lyrics of their songs. Your health and well-being could be improved by simply changing your preferences.

Ideally, the music you listen to when you feel like crap should not make you feel worse. You also don't want to listen to music that makes you feel depressed or like beating everybody up.

The music you listen to should make you feel happy and pull you out of a low state of being into a higher one. It's a bonus if you can dance to the music. Moving will help you to release whatever discomfort you're feeling and get in some chakra healing.

Affirmations are emotionally supportive and encouraging statements that you say to yourself or listen to on repeat as needed. They are the opposite of the destructive sayings, thoughts and feelings you might have, like "I am so dumb" or "I can't seem to do anything right" or "Nothing ever goes right for me."

If you're accustomed to speaking harshly of yourself, at first you might not believe the affirming words that you're replacing your harmful self-talk with are true. However, the more you say or think them, the more you'll believe them. Your mindset will adjust bringing you positive changes.

The best way to do affirmations is to record them in your own voice. Once you get used to your own tone, you will find that you prefer to listen to that over someone else's recordings. You can

---

[57] Cross, Alan. (2018, May 13). The great 440 Hz conspiracy, and why all of our music is wrong. *Global News*. Retrieved from https://globalnews.ca/news/4194106/440-hz-conspiracy-music/.

[58] Id.

record different sets of affirmations for different types of situations. For instance, I AM affirmations remind you of those characteristics you love about yourself and/or that you would like to cultivate in yourself.

If you're finding it challenging to create your own affirmations, know that whatever comes out of you is perfect. Still having trouble believing in yourself? Do your research to find affirmations and motivational literature that are available for personal use.

Smile (or laugh) even though you might be faking it. Eventually, it will become your default expression as you start to see the humor in your circumstances.

You're probably wondering how this can possibly be a mindfulness practice. Well, it is scientifically proven that smiling or laughing causes your brain to release feel-good hormones that help with stress management and attract good things to you.[59]

No one has to know you're smiling. Simply smiling on the inside tricks your brain into believing that you're in a better mood than your circumstances dictate. This better mood will radiate outward and create a chain effect that can move things around in your favor. The feel-good hormones that your brain releases shift your mindset/attitude so that you're able to find humor in what you're facing. You become relaxed and calm enough to figure a way out or through. You might feel silly at first. But after a while, it'll become easy and natural and you will actually begin to feel happy. I promise you!

All this to say that you can allow your circumstances and/or environment to keep you in the doldrums or you can choose to be happy. Not taking yourself and your circumstances too seriously helps. Seeing the humor in some of the situations you find yourself in helps you to overcome them much more quickly.

---

[59] The Health Benefits of Smiling. *SCL Health.* Retrieved from www.sclhealth.org/blog/2019/06/the-real-health-benefits-of-smiling-and-laughing.

Journaling is another practice that helps to release stress and improve your mood, among other things. You get to check in on yourself and your feelings as you write down your thoughts. By the time you're finished you feel better and/or have figured out a way to deal with whatever situation you're in. You gain insight because, as you write, things become clearer and solutions to your challenges show up. Maybe, you realize that you're worrying about nothing.

The good thing is that your journal entries will be available to you for future reference. Hopefully, rereading them won't make you cringe. If they do, there's your confirmation that you were stressed about nothing or have made progress.

At best, you might open a journal to a random page on a bad day and find an entry that reminds you that you are fully capable of handling whatever you are currently facing.

Along with journaling about your daily life, journaling about what you're grateful for helps you to remember that your life is not as bad as it seems. You could be grateful for a lesson learned, a thing/person in your life, an accomplishment, your family, a body part, and so on. A list of 3 to 5 things a day should be sufficient.

You also can journal about your dreams, what comes up in meditation, and your experiments on yourself using the tools and practices discussed in this book.

Baths, whether foot or full body, can be so uplifting and mellowing at the same time. It can be as simple as Epsom salts (or pink Himalayan salt) and a few drops of lavender oil in water as hot as you can take it. You can add herbs, candles, incense, music and crystals to the mix. It can be a simple bath just to relax, or a spiritual bath designed to help you to connect to yourself or release some type of trauma.[60]

You don't have to have a bathtub to take a bath. You can mix your bath solution in a bucket or basin (preferably made of material like stainless steel) and pour it on your body with the intention you have set.

Grounding (or earthing) is a process where you make direct contact with the earth by standing or walking on it with your bare feet, or by lying on it with bare skin or without interference from synthetic materials like plastic and rubber. Direct access to the earth exposes you to beneficial electrical charges.[61] You are disconnected from these electrical charges by the synthetic soles of your shoes. Synthetic materials insulate you from the natural healing electrical charges from the earth, which are a powerful antioxidant.[62]

Grounding helps with many challenges to our health and wellbeing, including the immune system, chronic fatigue, chronic pain, stress, anxiety and depression, and jetlag and sleep disorders.

If you don't have easy access to the bare earth (maybe because you live in an apartment building in New York City), you can purchase online things like grounding mats, sheets and socks.

Supercharged (Pyramid/Hydrogen) Water. Not to alarm you, but you live in a toxic soup of deuterium (heavy hydrogen). Heavy hydrogen is harmful for your body. It prematurely ages and deteriorates (get it?) our bodies. Do your research and you will find that deuterium damages your

---

[60] Hanekamp, Deborah. (2020). *Ritual Baths: Be Your Own Healer*. New York, NY: HarperCollins Books.

[61] Ober, Clinton, et al. (2014). *Earthing: The most important health discovery ever!* Basic Health Publications, Inc.

[62] *Id.*

mitochondria, which you inherited from your mother and which is important for your body to function optimally. You can do something about the effects of deuterium.

A simple way to deplete deuterium from your body and reduce its effects is to supercharge your water or make deuterium-depleted water. There are many devices currently available on the market that you can use for this process.

In the event that you cannot afford any of the devices, you can heat and cool distilled water 3, 6 or 9 times to improve the quality of the water you intake.[63] The process of heating and cooling the water charges it with the beneficial hydrogen your body needs to function optimally.

Detailed instructions on how to hydrogenate your water are provided by Bro. Hankh Rising Sun on his YouTube channel called Magnets Crystals and Pyramids.[64] For the heating and cooling process you will need a stainless-steel stock pot, a few gallons of distilled water, and a wooden spoon. Boil the distilled water in the pot. Then place the pot of boiling water into a sink of cold tap water. Do not put any of the cold tap water in the pot. Stir the hot water in the pot with the wooden spoon for 3 to 10 minutes. Repeat 3, 6 or 9 times.[65]

You can drink the supercharged water straight or use it to charge the spring water (1 ounce of supercharged water to a gallon of spring water) you use for cooking and drinking.

Show Yourself Love and Compassion. As a spiritual being having a human experience you have emotions and feelings like fear, stress, and anxiety. Although practice helps you to

---

[63] Magnets Crystals and Pyramids. How to Supercharge Drinking Water Part 1. https://www.youtube.com/watch?v=60bCP1INudk&t=732s.

[64] Id.

[65] Id.

become better at handling these emotions and feelings, you will slip up until you become a master at this. When you slip, take it easy.

You don't have to be one of those people who sits on a mountain meditating all of the time. You shouldn't be comparing your journey to anyone else's. Know that the slip-ups are a part of the process and are there to teach you about yourself. So, it is important to have love and compassion for yourself if/when you slip back into old patterns. It took a massive amount of conditioning to get you to fall into those patterns. This is why having a sense of humor is important. Have a good laugh (or cry), ask yourself what you're supposed to learn from this, and keep going.

Bodywork, through therapeutic touch and/or energy healing modalities like massage therapy, reiki, reflexology, craniosacral therapy, acupuncture and myofascial release, is necessary for maintaining health and well-being.

Despite the skepticism around these age-old practices, many people can attest to their lasting benefits. Bodywork can help to relieve aches, pain and tension, improve circulation, stimulate lymph flow, enhance immunity, and ease depression, for example.

Nutrients and Dietary Supplements

Some people should be taking dietary supplements and others should not. It all depends on where you live, the condition of the soil where the food you eat is grown, the kinds of activities you engage in, and your dietary choices.[66] Dr. Pookrum advised that "ethnicity determines what minerals and vitamins [to use]."[67]

These days, you don't have to visit a doctor's office to get blood work to determine whether you're deficient in any nutrient. You can access companies through an online search that allow you to order your own lab tests at a low cost.

You should be getting your nutrients from the food and herbs that you intake. If you cannot and are deficient, your supplements should not be genetically engineered or contain additives like toxic chemicals and oils, soy, sugar, gluten, dairy and corn. It is worth the money to buy a quality supplement. Always read the labels even if you're purchasing a better quality brand.

Below are some essential nutrients that you might have to supplement depending on your lifestyle and living environment, along with some of their nicknames and their commonly known benefits. I have experienced their benefits through my own use. You can do your own research and consult with your physician to learn more about them and to determine whether you should be taking any of them.

Vitamin A is called the "vision vitamin." It supports immune function, eye health, fetal development, reproduction and cell growth.

Foods containing Vitamin A include dark leafy greens, melons, fruits, pumpkin, parsley, sweet potato, okra, dandelion,

---

[66] Pookrum, Jewel. (1993). Vitamins and Minerals from A to Z with Ethno-Consciousness, p. 94. Atl. Ga.: J.E.W.E.L. Publications, Inc.

[67] Id.

watercress, dairy, liver and fish. Supplementation is recommended if you're on a completely meatless diet.

Vitamin B12 (one of the "energy vitamins"[68]) helps you to maintain healthy nerve and blood cells, as well as to prevent anemia from malformed red blood cells. B12 may also help to improve your mood and depression symptoms, and boost your energy. This means that it can help you to feel good.

B12 is found in animal products, as well as bananas and wheat germ.

Vitamin C (or ascorbic acid) is the "repair vitamin." It is an antioxidant that helps with the growth, development and repair of body tissues, including the bones, skin and blood vessels. It helps you to process protein, produce collagen and with adrenal function, as well as to protect your immune system and keep you disease-free.

As vitamin C helps your body to absorb and benefit from iron, take your iron supplement with a supplement or food containing vitamin C, like an orange.

You can get vitamin C from fruits and vegetables like citrus fruits, cherries, asparagus, avocado, guavas, kiwi, mangos, mustard greens, turnip greens, strawberries, red and green peppers, tomatoes, cantaloupe, broccoli and spinach.

Vitamin D (the "sunshine vitamin") is an antioxidant that helps your body to absorb calcium and phosphorus. A vitamin D

---

[68] The other "energy vitamins" make up the remainder of the B-Complex vitamins. They include B1 (thiamine), B2 (riboflavin), B3 (niacin), B5 (pantothenic acid), B6 (pyridoxine), B7 (biotin), and B9 (folate/folic acid). They each have their specific functions. Overall, they are important for estrogen regulation, stress response and cognitive functioning.

deficiency can lead to bone abnormalities like osteoporosis and other diseases. It supports your immune system to help prevent colds, the flu, and the coronavirus, and supports the health of your heart, hormones and thyroid, among other things.

Like B12, vitamin D helps to regulate your mood and improve anxiety and depression. Intaking it during stressful times could therefore be beneficial for you.

Vitamin D is called the "sunshine vitamin" because your skin produces it when your body is exposed to the sun's rays. In fact, the sun is the best source of vitamin D. The type of vitamin D produced by the skin is called vitamin D3. If you live in an environment where you have daily access to the sun's rays year-round and you take advantage of that, you're lucky and are probably not deficient in vitamin D.

People who live in colder climates may be deficient for obvious reasons and should supplement. For maximum benefit and absorption, the supplement should be vitamin D3, and it must be taken with vitamin K2, which helps your body to absorb D3 and is important for bone metabolism, blood coagulation, healthy blood vessels and in pregnancy.

It is scientifically proven that exposure to the sun "increases pineal gland activity, endurance, vitamin D, energy (increased glycogen stores in the liver), melanin secretion, strength, melatonin and serotonin, balance of stress, sex hormones and oxygen supply to the blood," and "decreases free radicals, respiratory rate, bone loss, lactic acid in the blood following exercise, diseases, blood pressure, fatigue and depression, blood sugar, and diastolic (resting heart rate)."[69]

The amount of daily sun exposure recommended is based on skin color, the amount of skin exposed, and the time of day. The more skin exposed the better, and preferably between 11 a.m.

---

[69] Afrika, Llaila O. (2009). *African Holistic Health*, p. 325. Astoria, NY: Seaburn Books.

and 3 p.m., according to the guidelines. Do your research to find what works for you.

Research has shown that the black pigmentation produced by melanin protects melanin-dominant people from the sun's ultraviolet rays.[70] Some seem to have interpreted this to mean that people with higher levels of melanin cannot absorb enough vitamin D from the sun.[71] Don't allow this to deter you from getting your vitamin D from the sun if you can.

Sunscreen is currently recommended for all during exposure to sunlight. While I am not advocating for or against sunscreen, it is notable that this recommendation is based on studies of the effects on skin of "artificial infrared radiation."[72] In other words, people in the study were not exposed to natural sunlight.

In fact, it has been known since at least 1968 that, early morning and late afternoon sun exposure can naturally prevent damage to and repair the human body.[73]

Vitamin D can be found in animal and plant sources. Fatty fish like salmon, sardines and egg yolk naturally contain vitamin D. You also can get vitamin D from dandelion greens, lettuce, sweet potatoes and watercress.

Vitamin E is an antioxidant that helps with immunity and fertility. It is found in sprouted seeds like sunflower seeds, pumpkin seeds, almonds and hazelnuts. It is also found in olive oil,

---

[70] Afrika, Llaila O. (2009). *Melanin: What Makes Black People Black*, p. 27. Long Island City, NY: Seaburn Books.

[71] Wilson, D.R. (2020, April 7). The Benefits of Vitamin D. *Healthline*. Retrieved from https://www.healthline.com/health/food-nutrition/benefits-vitamin-d

[72] Barolet, D, et al. (2016). Infrared and skin: Friend or foe. Journal of Photochemistry & Photobiology, B: Biology 155 (2016 78-85, 80.

[73] Id., 81.

tomatoes, avocado, green leafy vegetables, sweet potatoes, asparagus, and broccoli.

Vitamin K is important for bone (calcium) metabolism, blood coagulation, healthy blood vessels and a healthy pregnancy. There is K1 from plants and K2 from animals.

Green leafy vegetables, asparagus, brussels sprouts, cabbage and broccoli contain K1. Vitamin K2 is found in animal liver and fermented foods. Healthy gut bacteria in your large intestine produce vitamin K2.

A vitamin D3 supplement must be taken with vitamin K2 to fully benefit from the D3. Otherwise, you're wasting your money.

Iron is important for making blood and for oxygenation of the body as it helps it to transport red blood cells throughout your body. The amount of iron you might need depends on factors like age and sex, which drive things like whether you menstruate, and so on. In addition, you must take iron with vitamin C (juice or fruit) to better absorb the iron.

You can get iron from animal sources and from plants. Plants containing iron include spinach, turnip greens, walnuts, sunflower and sesame seeds, pumpkins, prunes, pears, bananas, avocados, almonds, apricots and peaches.

Magnesium is a mineral that is important in the function of more than 600 enzyme reactions within the body that deal with multiple processes including energy, stress, muscle maintenance, and sleep.

Although magnesium is found in many foods, including almonds, avocado, coriander, cooked dark green leafy greens, flax seeds, pumpkin seeds, cooked quinoa and seaweed, it is said to be the most common mineral deficiency in humans.

Zinc is another mineral that's supposed to be helpful for stress and disease management and prevention because it helps with the development and function of immune cells. It's involved in hundreds of enzyme reactions, hormone function, nerve and digestive function, and is antibacterial and anti-inflammatory.

You could be zinc-deficient if you get colds often or have changes in your senses of taste and smell.

Since your body doesn't produce zinc, you have to get it from food or supplements. Foods containing zinc include kelp, pumpkin, sunflower seeds, green leafy vegetables, nuts, legumes, and red meat.

Chlorophyll is the green pigment in plants that helps them to transform sunlight into food through photosynthesis.

Chlorophyll is beneficial for humans because it contains vitamins and antioxidants that stimulate your immunity, cleanse your intestines, and increase your energy, among other things.

You can enrich your drinking water with liquid chlorophyll to support your intake of leafy greens and green vegetables and to help to flush out toxins.

Liquid chlorophyll is also helpful for reducing body odors arising from the digestive tract. For this reason, it is considered to be a natural deodorant.

Probiotics are live bacteria and yeast that are beneficial for your body and digestive system. You can take them to help relieve bloating and a sluggish digestive system. Probiotics also have many other benefits that you can research.

A biotic is a community of living organisms. On your skin and inside of your body are communities of living microorganisms called a microbiome. Your microbiome consists of yeast, bacteria, fungi and other organisms, some of which are harmful and others that are helpful. Some of these organisms live in your gut.

Intaking excess sugar and processed foods and insufficient fiber and leafy green vegetables, adversely affects your microbiome population and can cause a proliferation of the harmful microorganisms that deplete the beneficial microorganisms. Environmental toxins and certain medications, including antibiotics, are also harmful. Antibiotics cannot tell the difference between the harmful and beneficial organisms in your gut. You would therefore be doing yourself a favor if you make some adjustments in your diet.

Clearly, if your digestive tract is functioning well, that's one less source of stress. Foods that naturally contain probiotics are fermented fruits, vegetables and drinks like pickles and kombucha. You should look for options that contain no added sugar.

🕊 🕊 🕊

Healing Herbs

Herbs are plants with parts (roots, bark, leaves, fruit, seeds and/or flowers) that have been used for centuries for their healing properties. A quick search will reveal that scientists have done studies to prove the healing benefits of many of the herbs that are regularly available to us. Some of these are modified by pharmaceutical companies to create drugs to treat certain illnesses. For instance, star anise is used to make the drug known as Tamiflu.

Herbs can be made into teas, as well as ointments, syrups, poultices, seasonings, and tinctures.

This is a short list to give you an idea of some of the herbs that you can add to your cupboard. They each have unique benefits. All of them boost your immune system. For these herbs and those not on this list, you should do your research and/or consult with a certified herbalist based on your needs.

Ashwagandha is an herb used in Ayurvedic medicine to, among other things, balance the immune system and the reaction to stressors. It is an adaptogen, which means that it helps your body adapt to and/or resist stress. In other words, it gives you what you need, whether it's more sleep or an improved stress response.

Based on my own experience, this herb is very intelligent. For instance, if you are sleep-deprived it somehow recognizes that and will help you to have a good night's rest. So be careful to set your alarm if you take it for the first time during your work week and have to be up by a certain time in the morning.

Burdock Root contains antioxidants that, among other things, help to treat colds and gastrointestinal issues, and reduce fever. It also purifies your blood, heals skin issues and helps with lymphatic function.

Burdock root contains vitamins A, B1, B2, B3, C, F, as well as iron, calcium, choline, manganese and selenium.

Chlorella is a green freshwater algae. Among its many benefits, chlorella may support your immune system, detox your body of radiation, and boost your energy levels and mental function.

Elderberry is an antioxidant-rich plant (berries, bark, flowers and leaves) used for medicinal and culinary purposes. Elderberry may also help to improve your mood, fight colds and the flu, fight inflammation, and support your immune system.

Elderberries are high in vitamin C. They also are high in bioflavonoids, which build and strengthen tissue and cells. The syrup can help you to avoid and/or stop the progression of colds, the flu and allergies.

Moringa is called the "Tree of Life" and "Nature's Multivitamin" because it contains many vitamins and minerals, as well as protein and antioxidants in its leaves, bark, seeds and roots. Clearly, you don't have to eat meat for protein given that moringa and a few of the herbs on this list contain protein. Think about it. Where does the cow get its protein?

This herb also has antibacterial and antibiotic properties. Regular use of moringa leaves and bark in tea can help you to maintain your health and immunity because of all the nutrients it contains.

Moringa root, bark and flowers are not recommended for use by pregnant and nursing mothers because of certain chemicals in them. Consult with a certified herbalist to see if moringa is right for you.

Mullein helps you to soothe your mucous membranes and release mucus if you have bronchial and respiratory issues. People who develop respiratory symptoms from coronavirus can therefore benefit from using mullein.

Mullein contains vitamins B3 and C, potassium, manganese, zinc and magnesium.

🕊

Star Anise you may know as a spice that you add to certain foods and beverages. What may not be widely known is that star anise is synthesized and chemicalized by pharmaceutical companies to make the drug Tamiflu because it contains an antiviral, and other components that treat coughs and the flu.

As you can imagine, you can add star anise to the homemade elderberry syrup you make to get you through flu season.

🕊

Spirulina is a blue-green algae that grows in fresh and salt water. It contains many beneficial vitamins and minerals, as well as omega-3 and omega-6 fatty acids and protein. Among other things, it may help to regulate your immune system and support your mental health.

The vitamins and minerals in spirulina include vitamins B1 and E, choline and chromium.

🕊

Turmeric is the herb that gives curry powder its yellow color. It has many benefits including fighting inflammation, boosting immunity, easing symptoms of depression and body pain, alleviating musculoskeletal pain. It is also helpful for your skin.

Take turmeric with a little ginger or black pepper so that your body can absorb it and benefit from it.

🕊   🕊   🕊

Essential Oils

Essential oils are the oils of plant extracts. They are used to support health and well-being through aromatherapy, topical application, in baths or in food. They are also used in household cleaning products and cosmetics.

Essential oils can be used for stress relief and to improve your health. For instance, lavender and bergamot essential oils help to relieve stress symptoms, while sandalwood, rose and chamomile essential oils help to improve your mood. In addition, oil of oregano is a natural antibiotic that has been known to stop a respiratory infection in its tracks.

Make sure that the oil you use on your skin or internally is food or therapeutic grade.

Check to see whether your oils of choice have to be diluted before you intake or apply them to your skin. Essential oils are very potent and can irritate your skin or cause internal damage. Popular oils used for diluting essential oils are olive oil, coconut oil, jojoba oil and sweet almond oil. They are called carrier oils.

Sacred Plants

You have probably heard of people using sacred plants, like sage, to cleanse their spaces or in rituals. Often, the dried plant is wrapped in bundles, or mixed in with incense and resins. You may have also seen incense or resins being burned in churches and temples. This process is called smudging. [74]

Smudging cleanses people, places and/or things of non-beneficial energies they may have acquired from their environment. Basically, you set an intention and ignite your plant in a fire-proof container, allow the flames to go out so that the remaining ember smolders and smokes until it burns out. The smoke does the cleansing. This article goes into much more detail.[75]

Do your research and let your intuition be your guide as to how and when to use these plants.

Cedar is used for cleansing and protection from unwanted energies.

Sage is probably the most well-known smudge to people who are new to using plants for energy clearing. It is generally used to cleanse your space and aura of unwanted energies and to improve your mood. As sage does not discriminate in what types of energies it clears, burn palo santo afterwards to bring back in the high vibrational energies. Or you can just burn palo santo.

Palo Santo ("holy wood") is a plant that grows in certain South American countries. Dried sticks from the tree are burned to

---

[74] Smudging involves fire and smoke. Be mindful to have your windows open to release the smoke and do not leave the smoking smudge unattended. Asthma or other chronic respiratory conditions may be exacerbated by smoke inhalation.

[75] A Definition of Smudging. (2017, February 2016). *Indigenous Corporate Training Inc.* Retrieved from www.ictinc.ca/blog/a-definition-of-smudging.

clear unwanted energy and to help you with stress. Be sure to purchase sustainably harvested palo santo.

🕊

Yerba Santa leaves help with protection and purification, among other things.

🕊   🕊   🕊

Crystals

Crystals are communication devices that consist of mineral formations with organized molecular structures. The ancient pyramids of Egypt (and elsewhere) were the cell towers of their time that used copper and crystals to transmit information. Through the ages to modern times, crystals are used for religious and spiritual practices, communication, protection, and healing. Today, crystals are important components of devices like your computers, televisions, cell phones, lighters, watches, clocks and radios. The term LCD translates to liquid crystal display.

In *Rocks of Ages: Anu Edition*, Ras Ben Anu provides historical, scientific and spiritual information on crystals and how to use them.[76] The main reason you need crystals as a spiritual being is to raise your vibrational frequency, heal yourself, enhance your gifts, and to communicate with yourself and your Spirit Team.

Crystals have energy frequencies that resonate with the frequency of your chakras. Their potential frequency is most easily recognized based upon their color, which generally corresponds with your chakras. For instance, black and red crystals generally vibrate in sync with the root chakra. So, potentially, red and black crystals have a lower vibratory frequency than crown chakra crystals.

Each type of crystal has its own unique properties, and some crystals have similar properties. There are crystals that help to protect you from unwanted and low vibrational energies while raising your vibration. They support you in energetic healing, and some can even help with physical healing. Clearly, crystals can be used to help you to navigate stressful times and life in general.

Raw crystals are best to work with because they have not been manhandled and retain their natural look, feel and frequency. Tumbled crystals are traumatized by the process of making them

---

[76] Anu, Ras Ben. (2008). *Rocks of Ages: Anu Edition*. Philadelphia, PA: Those Four Sounds.

smooth and shiny. Their vibratory frequency is severely affected and they are not as useful for healing and connecting.

Whenever you get a new crystal, clean it before use because you don't know whose or what's energy signature they have picked up. The point is to clean the crystal of all frequencies that can affect its ability to use it effectively. Crystals can be cleaned by smudging with a palo santo stick, setting it out in the sun or moon light depending on the crystal, placing it in the earth, or holding it under running water depending on the crystal. Once cleansed, do not allow anyone else to use your crystals.

As not all crystals like to be in water, sunlight or moonlight, the easiest tool for cleansing them is smoke. Even easier is to use selenite (a crystal we'll discuss below), to cleanse and charge your crystals.

Follow your intuition as to which crystals you should work with. Otherwise, below are some powerful crystals that everyone should have in their arsenal.[77]

Amethyst is a high frequency purple quartz crystal that helps you to increase your frequency and the frequency of the energy in your space. Amethyst helps with the crown and third-eye chakras.

Aquamarine helps with throat chakra issues by helping you to communicate. It also helps with communicating from the heart.

Black Obsidian is basically hardened lava. This crystal is known to absorb and repel harmful energies, including from the

---

[77] See Appendix I for a list of some crystals based on the information in *Rocks of Ages: Anu Edition* by Ras Ben Anu.

people around you. It can be used for root and other chakra healing work.

≫

Black Tourmaline is a crystal that helps to protect you from harmful energies. It also is a grounding crystal. Use black tourmaline for root chakra healing work.

≫

Carnelian is highly recommended for sacral chakra healing work. As such, it helps to boost your creativity.

≫

Citrine is another quartz crystal that can help you to maintain confidence and self-esteem. It is mostly used for solar plexus chakra work.

≫

Clear Quartz is a very high vibrating crystal that amplifies the energy of other crystals. It can help you to de-clutter your mind, body and spirit and align with your higher self. It can be used for crown and other chakra healing work.

≫

Rose Quartz is the love crystal for its ability to open users up to unconditional love. It is used for heart chakra healing.

≫

Malachite is another heart chakra crystal. It works a little differently from the rose quartz in that it is more about helping the heart heal from traumas that make it difficult to connect with your heart. It can also protect from you harmful energies. The other thing about malachite is that it is copper, which is a conductor and a component of melanin and the pineal gland.

≫

Shungite, although not technically a crystal, is very high vibrating and is the best crystal for protecting yourself from low vibrational energy and radiation. It is a black mineraloid (consisting mostly of carbon) found only in the Russian village of Shunga in the Republic of Karelia in Russia since a meteorite chose Shunga as its resting place.[78]

Shungite is proven to protect wearers from electromagnetic radiation emitted by electronic devices and microwaves. Notably, shungite is used in Russia to protect cancer patients from the effects of radiation therapy and to help other patients to heal from cancer and other illnesses because it contains antioxidant fullerenes (special types of carbon molecules).[79]

Shungite can also provide spiritual and emotional protection and purification. It helps to cleanse toxic energy.[80]

Elite (silver or noble or Type 1 shungite) can be used to purify drinking water.[81]

Selenite is a high vibrating crystal that provides light and positive energy. It clears stagnant energy and helps to keep you and your space vibrating high. As you know, vibrating high is one of the ways that you can maintain a healthy immune system.

You also can use selenite to charge and cleanse your other crystals, and as a personal shield from unwanted energies.

Selenite is a crown chakra healing crystal. However, it can be used to help balance and harmonize all of your other chakras.

---

[78] Martino, R. (2011). *Shungite: Protection, Healing, and Detoxification.* Rochester, Vermont Healing Arts Press.

[79] Id.

[80] Id.

[81] Id.

What's Next...

In the next Chapter, I will introduce you to what you can do and use to protect yourself from harmful 5G radiation.

Chapter Thirteen: Protect Yourself from Harmful Electromagnetic Radiation and Other Low Vibrations

Recently, wireless technology was upgraded from 4G to 5G (the 5th generation of wireless technology). Towers for transmitting artificial electromagnetic waves have popped up around us adding more harmful radiation to our environments. This is different from your natural electromagnetic frequency.

If you do a search, you'll find that there are different opinions on whether artificial electromagnetic frequencies (EMF) emitted by 5G technology adversely affects our health. While some say there is no evidence of harm, others say the opposite. Some scientific studies have concluded that exposure to harmful EMF causes damage, including "triggers oxidative stress in various tissues [including mitochondrial DNA], causes significant changes in levels of blood antioxidant markers [and symptoms like] fatigue, headache, decreased learning ability, and cognitive impairment."[82] [83]

Now, as if increasing levels of artificial EMF is not enough to worry about, you are exposed daily to people, places and things whose vibrational frequency can negatively impact yours and stress you out. There are ways to protect yourself.

---

[82] Kivrak, E.G., et al. Effects of electromagnetic fields exposure on the antioxidant defense system. Journal of Microscopy and Ultrastructure 5 (2017) 167-176, 173.

[83] Shangcheng Xu, et al. Exposure to 1800 MHz radiofrequency radiation induces oxidative damage to mitochondrial DNA in primary cultured neurons. Brain Research. Vol. 1311, 22 January 2010, 189-196. https://doi.org/10.1016/j.brainres.2009.10.062.

Some crystals and metals, like copper, silver and gold, are effective tools that you can use to protect yourself from or limit your exposure to the effects of harmful EMF, people, places and things. Below, we will talk about some of these crystals and copper.

Shungite[84] is the best crystal for protecting yourself from harmful EMF. It is a black mineraloid (consisting mostly of carbon) found only in the Russian village of Shunga in the Republic of Karelia in Russia where to land.

Shungite is proven to protect wearers from electromagnetic radiation emanating from electronic devices and microwaves. Notably, shungite is used in Russia to protect cancer patients from the effects of radiation therapy and to help other patients to heal from cancer and other illnesses.[85]

Elite (silver or noble or Type 1 shungite) can be placed in drinking water to purify it of harmful bacteria.[86] You also should protect yourself when you're using your electronics by wearing or carrying a piece of shungite.

Black Obsidian is basically hardened lava. One of the things that it does is shield you from and cleanse your aura of harmful EMF.

Black Tourmaline protects you from and eliminates harmful energies (from EMF and people).

---

[84] Martino, R. (2011). *Shungite: Protection, Healing, and Detoxification.* Rochester, Vermont Healing Arts Press.

[85] Id.

[86] Id.

Orgonite is a device made of metals (like copper) and crystals – like the ones discussed above – encased in resin. It is designed to protect, balance and organize your life force energy (chi or orgone). [87]

Wearing and placing orgonite around you can protect your person and home from the effects of EMF. Orgonite also helps clear other types of harmful energies, balance your mood, purify the air, and improve your sleep, among other things. [88]

Selenite helps users to remain calm and peaceful in the midst of chaos. Taking charge of how you show up in the world is one of the ways that you can maintain a healthy immune system. This doesn't mean that there's no place for righteous indignation in your life, however. It is important to speak up for yourself no matter how spiritual you are.

Copper is a trace mineral that's found in certain foods. It is also a metal that's used to make jewelry and as an electricity conductor, among other things. Copper's ability to block electromagnetic radiation is well known.

You can wear copper jewelry and purchase copper devices. Some companies also sell copper fabric, which can be used to fortify your home against 5G radiation.

A bonus of using copper is that it kills harmful bacteria.[89] For this you can store and drink your water from copper mugs and bottles.

---

[87] What is Orgonite? *Orgonise Yourself.* Retrieved from orgoniseyourself.com/how-orgonite-heals/

[88] Id.

[89] Yin, Fei, et al. (2019). Antiparasitic Effect of Copper Alloy Surface on *Cryptocaryon irritans* in Aquaculture of *Larimichthys crocea*. Appl Environ Microbiol. 85:e01982-18. https://doi.org/10.1128/AEM.01982-18. Retrieved from www.ncbi.nlm.nih.gov/pmc/articles/PMC6344632/#__ffn_sectitle.

Your skin might react to copper by turning green or breaking out in a rash. If this happens to you, it could be that your body needs to be cleansed of a build-up of toxins introduced into your body through your environment and food. You should be fine after doing a cleanse.

What's Next...

Now it's time to put whatever resonates with you into practice.

Have fun!

Conclusion

When I run after what I think I want,
my days are a furnace of distress and
anxiety. If I sit in my own place, what
I need flows to me, without pain.
From this I understand that what I
want also wants me, is looking for and
attracting me.

There is a great secret in this for
anyone who can grasp it.

--Rumi

Spirituality is about tapping into yourself. It invites you to go into yourself for your answers and guidance. The more you do so, the more of yourself you welcome in and become.

On the other hand, religion requires you to rely on others – people, places, things – outside of you to tell you who you are and how to be.

When you're challenged, go within first, trust the guidance and knowing that you receive and remember, and follow that. This doesn't mean that you can't ask others how they handled the same challenge. Either you'll confirm that your approach is right for you or receive some support or useful information. Having confidence in your inner guidance and releasing any guilt you may feel for not following your parents' or friends' advice, invites your meta-Self to reveal more and more of itself to you.

Do yourself a favor and start to work on remembering how to tap in to you again so that you get the answers you're looking for. They're already coming through. You just don't know how to recognize them as such. This is where meditation comes in.

Take action to improve your life beyond material things like a new car or the latest designer offerings and/or what the celebrities are doing. They are all distractions that you soon tire of and realize that you're in the same position where you started; completely stressed out and frustrated with your life.

On its face, it might seem as if being spiritual means you're giving up free will. Free will is truth in the sense that you have the option to follow your inner guidance over your ego. If for you, free will currently means that you're free to do what you want, notice how much chaos and stress you encounter when you don't allow yourself to be guided.

Feel free to experiment with following your intuition, and watch high vibrational magic come into your life. You, your circumstances and relationships, and your environments will change in surprisingly delightful ways. You'll still have challenges. Just not like before.

Whether you listen to your ego or intuition, magic will occur. It's up to you if your magic produces more stress and strain for you instead of ease and joy. You came here knowing this. Unfortunately, the education system and your conditioning quickly dumbed you down from that knowing.

The work to get back on your true path can be confusing and tiresome because you're stepping into territory that your ego is not comfortable with. Concepts like "being spirit-led" and "you create your reality" can be difficult to grasp in the beginning. Just know that, if you're serious about making profound change in your life, you'll be led to the people, places and things who are supposed to help and mentor you. Acknowledge that you're stuck and ask your Spirit Team for help. They'll guide you to your teacher.

Don't feel bad that it might have taken you this long to get to this point. It happened to all of us.

What's Next...

Like I said before, have fun with it!

Appendix I: <u>Table of Crystals</u>

This is a list of some of the better-known crystals, along with their mineral components and some of their known properties. The mineral components were taken from Rocks of Ages: Anu Edition.[90]

CRYSTAL	MINERAL COMPONENTS ESSENTIAL FOR LIFE	SOME BENEFICIAL PROPERTIES
Agate	Oxygen, Silicon	Grounding; Stabilizing; Soothing; and Stress-Relieving. *Properties may differ depending on the type of agate.
Amethyst	Oxygen, Silicon	Elevating; Helps with Relaxation and Finding Inner Peace; Tap into Intuition.
Apatite	Calcium, Chlorine, Hydrogen, Oxygen, Phosphorus	Elevating; Brings Clarity to Self-Expression.
Aragonite	Calcium, Carbon, Oxygen	Release low vibrational energy; anger; anxiety and fear.
Aventurine	Oxygen, Silicon	Neutral; Calming; Heart-opening.
Azurite	Copper, Hydrogen, Oxygen,	Elevating; Enhances Creativity and Inner Wisdom; Helps to

[90] Anu, Ras Ben. (2008). *Rocks of Ages: Anu Edition.* Philadelphia, PA: Those Four Sounds.

CRYSTAL	MINERAL COMPONENTS ESSENTIAL FOR LIFE	SOME BENEFICIAL PROPERTIES
		Heal Communication Issues.
Calcite	Calcium, Carbon, Oxygen,	Release creative blockages and toxic emotions. *Comes in different colors with each color having different properties.
Carbon Quartz	Carbon,	Highly Grounding.
Carnelian	Oxygen, Silicon	Grounding; Boosts Self-Esteem and Self-Confidence: Helps you to Tap Into Your Passion.
Celestite	Oxygen	Elevating; Calming; Helps the Body Relax and Rest; Stress and Anxiety Relieving.
Chalcopyrite	Copper	Align chakras; Creativity.
Chrysocolla	Copper, Hydrogen, Oxygen, Silicon	Neutral; Energizing and Motivating; Calming.
Citrine	Oxygen, Silicon	Uplifting; Confidence Booster; Positivity; Optimism.
Copper	Copper	Neutral.

CRYSTAL	MINERAL COMPONENTS ESSENTIAL FOR LIFE	SOME BENEFICIAL PROPERTIES
Diamond	Carbon	Emotional Growth; Self-love; Enhance Inner Vision.
Epidote	Calcium, Hydrogen, Silicon,	Absorb Anger, Resentment, Hurt, Confusion, Frustration and Disappointment; Heart Opening; Trust Building.
Fluorite	Calcium, Fluorine,	Elevating; Cleanses and Purifies the Heart Chakra; Opens the Third-Eye Chakra.
Hematite	Iron, Oxygen	Grounding; Balancing; Clears and Activates the Root Chakra; Calms the Mind and Spirit.
Herkimer Diamonds, Matrix of	Carbon	Highly Elevating; Amplifier of High Vibrations; Healing; Attuning
Jet	Coal	Highly Grounding; Draws out Low Vibrations; Purifying; Luck; Enhances Transformation; Clarity.
Kyanite	Oxygen, Silicon	Elevating.
Labradorite	Calcium, Oxygen, Silicon, Sodium	Encourages Limitless Expansion.

CRYSTAL	MINERAL COMPONENTS ESSENTIAL FOR LIFE	SOME BENEFICIAL PROPERTIES
Lapis Lazuli	Lazurite	Deepens Connection to Self; Opens Third Eye Chakra; Confidence & Authenticity.
Lepidolite	Hydrogen, Lithium, Oxygen, Potassium, Silicon	Mood Stabilizing; Balances Mind and Spirit.
Malachite	Carbon, Copper, Hydrogen, Oxygen	Neutral; Transforming; Supports Growth; Heart Chakra Healing.
Marcasite	Iron, Sulfur	Elevating; Inspires Creativity; Aid in Introspection.
Moqui Marbles	Iron, Sandstone	Grounding; Magnetizes and Fortifies the Aura.
Moldavite	Oxygen, Silicon, Aluminum	Highly elevating; Magnify Vibration; Past Life Clearing; Transforming.
Moonstone	Sodium, Potassium, Aluminum	Neutral; Helps with Sleep; Helps Align with Higher Self and Purpose.
Obsidian	Silicon	Highly Grounding; Helps Overcome Challenges; Cleanses and Blocks Low Vibrational Energy.

CRYSTAL	MINERAL COMPONENTS ESSENTIAL FOR LIFE	SOME BENEFICIAL PROPERTIES
Onyx	Oxygen, Silicon	Highly Grounding; Soothing; Brings Harmony; Protective.
Opal	Hydrogen, Oxygen, Silicon	Highly elevating; Boosts Creativity; Inspires Originality.
Pyrite	Iron, Sulfur	Grounding; Symbol of Wealth and Good Luck; Business Decision-Making; Protection.
Quartz	Oxygen, Silicon	Elevating.
Selenite	Selenium	Highly elevating; Energy Clearing; Uplifting; Cleansing; Charge Other Crystals.
Smoky Quartz	Carbon	Grounding; Helps you Let Go and Move On; Cleansing and Purifying.
Sodalite	Chlorine, Oxygen, Silicon, Sodium	Communication; Calming and Soothing; Harmonizing
Tiger's Eye	Oxygen, Silicon	Emotional Balancing; Attract Wealth; Confidence; Courage.
Topaz	Oxygen, Silicon	Promotes Forgiveness and Truth; Soothes; Heals; Recharges.

CRYSTAL	MINERAL COMPONENTS ESSENTIAL FOR LIFE	SOME BENEFICIAL PROPERTIES
Tourmaline	Hydrogen, Oxygen,	Grounding; Protective; Fosters Compassion and Calm.
Tourmaline (Black)	Iron, Sodium	Highly Grounding; Protective; Blocks Low Vibrations.
Tourmaline (Green)		Grounding; Stimulates Happiness and Joy; Heart Healing; Good for Herbalists.
Turquoise	Copper, Oxygen, Phosphorus	Grounding; Calming; Promotes Open Communication; Removes low vibrational Energy and Replaces it with Positive Vibes.

Appendix II: <u>Resources</u>

This is a short list of available resources.

<u>WEBSITES</u>

Education   spiritualascensionuniversity.com
thespiritdoulaacademy.com
columbianxchange.com
llailaafrika.com

Crystals   zoeessentials.com
rasben.com
columbianxchange.com

Food & Herbs   llailaafrika.com
drsebiscellfood.com
zoeessentials.com

Cosmic Tools   orgone4you.com
sacredwoodessence.com
zoeessentials.com

<u>COACHING & COUNSELING</u>

Health & Wellness   beboundless.com

Relationships   relationshipalchemy.org

Spiritual Path Guidance   thespiritdoula.com
mentalalchemy.com
beboundless.com

Astrology   hoodmystic.com
sistarmyrah.com

Chakra Healing   thechakradoc.com

S.E.X. Healing	nikkiexperience.com
Reiki & More	thewellnessgalaxy.com
	beboundlessllc.com

YOUTUBE CHANNELS

blackmagik363
Black Yogi Nico Marie
Blessed Ascensions
Conjure Queen
DRA Wise TheHealingCoach
Dream Wise
growwithjo
Hood Mystic
Khemetic Centered Living
Magnets Crystals And Pyramids
Professor Melanie, The Spirit Doula
Soitis Written
The SOUL Mentor

Appendix III: <u>Chakra Healing</u>[91]

CHAKRA: ROOT

Color & Element: Red; Earth

Survival, security, stability.

About feeling safe and secure in our foundation.

Blockage causes: ungroundedness, fear, insecurity re basic needs.

Physical: colon, bladder, lower back, legs and/or feet issues.

Psychic: poor boundaries, disconnect from the body, fears, anxiety disorders.

Sound: LAM

Action: I AM

Crystals: Black tourmaline, black obsidian, hematite, black kyanite, nuumite, shungite, red jasper, garnet, ruby.

---

[91] Credit for this chakra healing information goes to Prof. Melanie John a/k/a The Spirit Doula.

CHAKRA: SACRAL

Color & Element: Orange; Water

Authentic creation, creator, soul fire, sexuality.

About creative & sexual energy, having healthy boundaries, connections w/others & new experiences.

Blockage causes: issues with creative and sexual energy.

Physical: fibroids, reproductive disorders, menstrual difficulties, sexual dysfunction.

Psychic: feeling emotional instability, uninspired creatively, fear change, lack desires, addiction like behaviors.

Sound: VAM

Action: I FEEL

Crystals: Carnelian, orange calcite, red jasper.

CHAKRA: SOLAR PLEXUS

Color & Element: Yellow; Fire

Power, self-worth, self-esteem, self-confidence. Controls the ability to be confident and in control of your life.

About metabolic, digestive & stomach-related; source of personal power.

Blockage causes: inability to be confident & in control of your life, always apologizing.

Physical: digestive & metabolic systems imbalanced – diabetes, hypoglycemia, eating disorders.

Psychic: low self-esteem, difficulties making decisions, anger/control issues.

Sound: RAM

Action: I DO

Crystals: Citrine, Tiger's eye, pyrite, amber, topaz yellow jasper.

CHAKRA: HEART

Color & Element: Green; Air

Love, joy, inner peace

Where physical & spiritual meet.

About ability to love & awakening of spiritual awareness & governs chest organs.

Blockage causes: grief, anger, jealousy, fear of betrayal, hatred of self & others.

Physical: heart and circulatory issues or lung and breathing issues.

Psychic: depression, loneliness, judgmental feelings, jealousy blocking opportunities to love.

Sound: YAM

Action: I LOVE

Crystals: Malachite, amazonite, chryscolla, green aventurine, fluorite, rose quartz, pink tourmaline, emerald, unakite, rhodonite, garnet and ruby.

CHAKRA: THROAT

Color & Element: Blue; Ether – combo of air & water

Communication, speaking the truth, self-expression of feelings, holding secrets, ability to truly hear.

About speaking and listening; speaking & properly communicating inner truths and feelings; ability to listen to self & others.

Blockage from holding in emotions & not speaking your truth.

Blockage causes: fear of speaking/judgment, difficulty expressing feelings, shyness, weak voice, talkative, struggle to listen/hear others.

Physical: sore throat, thyroid issues, neck & shoulder stiffness, tension headaches.

Psychic: always apologizing (like sacral & solar plexus).

Sound: HAM

Action: I SPEAK

Crystals: Turquoise, aquamarine, blue kyanite, blue apatite, blue topaz, blue lace agate, Celestine, larimar.

CHAKRA: THIRD EYE

Color & Element: Dark Blue; Transcendence, the Mind

Link between inner and outer worlds.

Intuition, imagination, wisdom, ability to think & make decisions, love, joy, inner peace, memory.

About your intuition, perception, connecting to higher and lower self and intuitive clarity.

Blockage causes: inability to dream and meditate or connect to spiritual gifts.

Physical: headaches, dizziness, vision problems, memory issues, brain health issues, endocrine problems, brain fog.

Psychic: blocked lower chakras, trouble tapping into & trusting intuition, judgmental, dismissive, introverted, anxiety, depression.

Sound: ONG

Action: I SEE

Crystals: Lapis lazuli, sodalite, azurite, blue kyanite, labradorite, sapphire.

CHAKRA: CROWN

Color & Element: Purple; Nothing & Everything

Cognition, connection to spirituality and Higher Self and life's purpose.

About connection to the universe and spiritual growth; moving past material needs and accessing utmost clarity and enlightened wisdom while remaining grounded.

Blockage from feelings of isolation and disconnection from everyone & everything.

Blockage causes: feeling out of sorts; stress on body and mind.

Physical: if overactive, disconnect from physical body and earthly matters so that you lack empathy and care for self and others.

Psychic: hinder ability to let go of material needs, letting go of ego due to spiritual heights.

Sound: Whatever comes to you in the moment

Action: I KNOW

Crystals: Amethyst, moonstone, howlite, labradorite, lepidolite, clear quartz, selenite, rainbow fluorite, serpentine, desert rose.

Bibliography

Afrika, Llaila O. (2009). African Holistic Health. Astoria, NY: Seaburn Books.

Afrika, Llaila O. (2009). Melanin: What Makes Black People Black, p. 27. Long Island City, NY: Seaburn Books.

Anthony, K. (2020). Astrology Explained: How to Use Imagination to Understand Astrology at an Intimate Level. Monee, IL: https://columbianxchange.com.

Anthony, K. (2020). Chakra Nova: You Are the Book. Middletown, DE: https://columbianxchange.com.

Anthony, K. (2020). How to Read Natal Charts Easily and Effectively; Understanding your birth chart in your own language. A workbook. San Bernardino, CA: https://columbianxchange.com.

Anu, Ras Ben. (2008). Rocks of Ages: Anu Edition. Philadelphia, PA: Those Four Sounds.

Arewa, Caroline S. (1998). Opening to Spirit: Contacting the Healing Power of the Chakras & Honouring African Spirituality. Baltimore, MD: Afrikan World Books.

Bertrand, Azra, et al. (2017). Womb Awakening: Initiatory Wisdom from the Creatrix of All Life. Rochester, Vermont: Bear & Company.

Bird, Stephanie R. (2009). A Healing Grove: African Tree Remedies and Rituals for Body and Spirit. Chicago, IL: Lawrence Hill Books.

Collins, Selwyn A. (2011). The EartHeart Knows. Brooklyn, NY: https://eartheartknows.selco2000.com.

Cooper, D.A. (1997). God Is a Verb: Kabbalah and the Practice of Mystical Judaism, pp. 127-9. New York, NY: Riverhead Books.

Dalai Lama, et al. (2016). The Book of Joy: Lasting Happiness in a Changing World. New York: Penguin Random House.

Foundation for Inner Peace. (2007). A Course in Miracles: Combined Volume.

Freke, T. and Gandy, P. (1997). The Hermetica: The Lost Wisdom of the Pharoahs. Kindle Edition: Timothy Freke Publications.

Freke, T. and Gandy, P. (2001). Jesus and the Lost Goddess: The Secret Teachings of the Original Christians. New York, NY: Three Rivers Press.

Hall, Judy. (2003). The Crystal Bible. London, UK: Octopus Books.

Hall, Judy. (2009). The Crystal Bible 2. London, UK: Octopus Books.

Hall, Judy. (2012). The Crystal Bible 3. London, UK: Octopus Books.

Hanekamp, Deborah. (2020). Ritual Baths: Be Your Own Healer. New York, NY: HarperCollins Books.

Hay, Louise. (1982). Heal Your Body: The Mental Causes for Physical Illness and the Metaphysical Way to Overcome Them. U.S.: Hay House, Inc.

Ma'at em Maakheru Amen. (2017). UnWOMBded: Unlocking the Universal Uterus. Middletown, DE: The Maat Foundation.

Ma'at em Maakheru. (2017). Whatz In Your Womb? Middleton, DE: The Maat Foundation.

Martino, R. (2011). Shungite: Protection, Healing, and Detoxification. Rochester, Vermont: Healing Arts Press.

Ober, Clinton, et al. (2014). Earthing: The most important health discovery ever! Basic Health Publications, Inc.

Pookrum, Jewel. (1993). Vitamins and Minerals from A to Z with Ethno-Consciousness. Yelm, WA: J.E.W.E.L. Publications, Inc.

Ruiz, Don Miguel. (1997). The Four Agreements: A Practical Guide to Personal Freedom. San Rafael, CA: Amber-Allen Publishing.

Ruiz, Jr., Don Miguel. (2016). The Mastery of Self: A Toltec Guide to Personal Freedom. San Antonio, TX: Hierophant Publishing.

Acknowledgments

I couldn't have written this Manual without the promptings from my Spirit Team. I am so grateful to Mama Universe and my ancestors. I am taken care of beyond my belief during this process of transformation I am experiencing.

Although we often give parents a bad rap for being parents, learning more about my parents' early lives this past year has convinced me that the bottom line is that these two magnificent people survived a whole lot of "ish" so that I can be here at this time. That goes for whoever is reading this as well. Regardless of what they might have done or not done, you're here and you can heal. Having said all of that, I am beyond thankful for the parents I chose.

I am so, so, so grateful to Selwyn Collins for being my able guide and companion over what I know is lifetimes, and for writing my Foreword. Our relationship/friendship continues to mean so much to me. You are one of my biggest and best teachers. I will always love you.

Thank you to my family and friends for tolerating me practicing on them what is being channeled through me. I know you wanted to shut me down many times, but I know you heard me.

The Spirit Doula and Spiritual Ascension University were brought to me when I didn't know how much I needed them. I am grateful to Melanie John for sharing truth, which has helped me to fill in blocks of information I didn't know I needed for this Manual.

I also want to acknowledge Teri Gandy-Richardson for offering the course that helped me to learn about yoga on a deeper level.

Finally, I am grateful for all of the experiences that propelled me to this point. I will keep walking even though I have no idea where I'm ending up.

About the Author

Looking back, Gillian was a born coach. While growing up she wanted to help people heal and find equilibrium in their lives. She was on a mission to become a psychiatrist or psychologist. Instead, she ventured into the legal field and became an attorney.

During her 10+ years in the legal field, Gillian experienced first-hand the systems that throw us off-balance, force us to seek guidance outside of ourselves, and place us in survival mode. She also developed her communication and many other skills, including a desire to pursue her purpose.

While in the legal field, Gillian became a Certified Holistic Health Coach through the Institute for Integrative Nutrition. Just before the 2020 pandemic, she left corporate America and stepped out on her 'yellow brick road,' having no idea where this new path would lead. In 2020, she launched her coaching practice, and in 2021 she became a Reiki practitioner.

Gillian is constantly reminded of her soul's mission to coach people on how to live and work in resonance with their Spirit, heal from the trauma of living in survival mode, and thrive.

Her goal is to encourage her clients to embrace and trust their inner guidance.

Visit the author's website at beboundlessllc.com.

www.ingramcontent.com/pod-product-compliance
Lightning Source LLC
Chambersburg PA
CBHW060534130626
46553CB00002B/746